THE WORLD'S BEST TRAVEL GAMES

Sheila Anne Barry

Illustrated by Doug Anderson

Sterling Publishing Co., Inc. **New York**

By the Same Author

Super-Colossal Book of
Puzzles, Tricks & Games
Test Your Wits
Tricks & Stunts to
Fool Your Friends
The World's Best
Party Games

Library of Congress Cataloging-in-Publication Data

Barry, Sheila Anne.
  The world's best travel games.

  Includes index.
  Summary: Presents over seventy games to play when
travelling in a car, bus, plane, or train, walking
through long corridors, sitting in terminals, or waiting
in restaurants.
  1. Games for travelers—Juvenile literature.
[1. Games for travelers. 2. Games] I. Anderson, Doug,
1919–   ill. II. Title.
GV1206.B375   1987   794   87-7065
ISBN 0-8069-6550-9
ISBN 0-8069-6551-7 (lib. bdg.)

ISBN 0-8069-6776-5 (pbk.)

Copyright © 1987 by Sterling Publishing Co., Inc.
387 Park Avenue South, New York, N.Y. 10016
Distributed in Canada by Sterling Publishing
% Canadian Manda Group, P.O. Box 920, Station U
Toronto, Ontario, Canada M8Z 5P9
Distributed in Great Britain and Europe by Cassell PLC
Artillery House, Artillery Row, London SW1P 1RT, England
Distributed in Australia by Capricorn Ltd.
P.O. Box 665, Lane Cove, NSW 2066
Manufactured in the United States of America

Contents

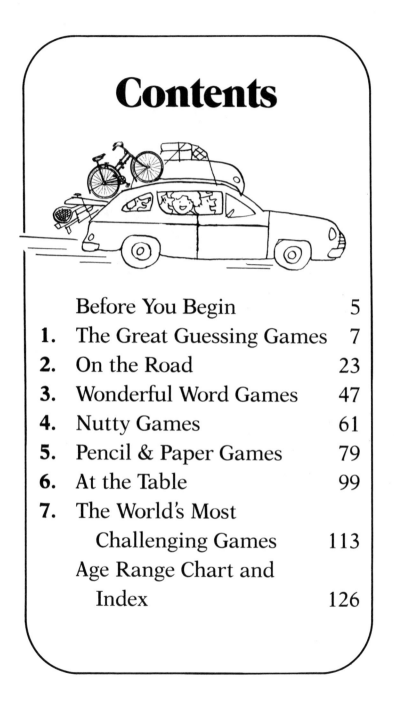

	Before You Begin	5
1.	The Great Guessing Games	7
2.	On the Road	23
3.	Wonderful Word Games	47
4.	Nutty Games	61
5.	Pencil & Paper Games	79
6.	At the Table	99
7.	The World's Most Challenging Games	113
	Age Range Chart and Index	126

To my mother
—one of the world's best travellers—
who taught me what fun it is
to go places and play games
with love

Before You Begin

If it's true that half the fun of going places is getting there, then it's certainly important to enjoy the time spent on the plane or train, in the car or the bus, sitting in the terminal, walking through long corridors or waiting for waiters who don't wait on you and friends who dally at the table.

Sometimes it's easy to enjoy all of it, because there are interesting people to look at, because the atmosphere is different and exciting, or because there's so much new experience to think about.

At other times, it's not so easy. Driving on expressways, thruways, turnpikes, freeways, autobahns—whatever you call them—bores me silly. And jetting through the blue and white skies has always left me hungry for more than the entertainment or snack that the airlines offer. That is where these games come in.

Some of them just help you open your eyes to what is actually going on around you (such as the car games starting on page 24). Some of them exercise your mental muscles as you play with words or sounds or cards. Some of them take you deep into your own mind, like "Essences," my personal favorite. Some of them bring you a warmer, happier feeling about the people around you—like singing silly songs (no auto trip was ever possible in my family without that!).

Most of the games can be played anywhere—in car or bus, plane or train—walking, waiting or whiling away the hours over coffee, tea or Chinese noodles. For that reason, we didn't want to limit them by placing them in separate chapters ("For the Plane" or

"For the Bus," "For Waiting Rooms" or "For the Air-line Cafeteria"). Therefore, for each game, you'll find an emblem showing where it's possible to use it:

Car

Bus

Train

Plane

Walking

Waiting

Eating Out

and you'll be able to tell straight off whether it's a game that's right for you at that moment.

So—now to the games! Have a great trip!

__1__
The Great Guessing Games

Most of the games in this section are famous, and it's no wonder, because they get more interesting the more you play them.

All guessing games work the same way: one of the players thinks of a subject and the others guess what it is.

But the subject can be practically anything—the possibilities are endless! Once the players realize how wide open their choices are, and learn the tricks and shortcuts and strategies of guessing, the games can become challenging beyond belief.

I Spy

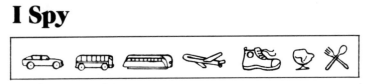

Players: 2 or more
Equipment: None
Preparation: None

The least complex of all the guessing games, this is a good quickie for playing when you don't have much time. It calls for no moving about, no great concentration, and the only requirement is that you stay in one place long enough to complete a round of the game.

First you choose a subject, which can be anything in full view of all the players. Then you reveal one characteristic of the subject. You could say, "I spy something red," or "I see something soft," or "I see something metal." But you don't say anything else about it.

The other player or players then start to guess what your subject is. Instead of answering just "yes" or "no," you answer according to how close they come—in space—to the subject.

For example, let's say you're on a plane and it's just before dinner. The subject you selected is the brown tie of the steward who is moving up and down the aisle of the plane, serving meals to passengers.

> YOU: I see something brown.
> CHARLIE: Is it your sweater?
> YOU (*glancing at the steward, who is all the way in the front of the plane loading up trays*): No, you're cold, very cold.

CHARLIE (*looking toward the front of the plane at a passenger close to the steward*): Is it that blond guy's leather jacket?

YOU (*anwering slowly, as the steward makes his way down the aisle towards you*): No, you're lukewarm. Actually, you're cold. . . . Yes, you're getting colder by the minute.

CHARLIE (*baffled*): What do you mean by *that*?

LINDA (*in the aisle seat, taking a tray from the steward and grinning—she thinks she knows*): Is it the steward's big brown eyes?

YOU: No, but you're blazing hot.

Well, you get the idea. Charlie or Linda will probably guess that your subject has something to do with the steward, and the round is soon over. Just in time, or the food on those trays would get cold. Sometimes you *need* a short game.

Name That Tune

Players: 2 or more
Equipment: None
Preparation: None

Here's a classic game you can play just about any-where—indoors or out, riding, walking or sitting—and it's also quick and easy. All you need is something to tap with and something to tap against. A knuckle or a fingernail will do for the tapper. A book, tabletop, dashboard or watch crystal will do for the tappee. Or you could just clap.

First you tap out the rhythm of a song. Then your opponents need to guess what the song is. Start with simple, well-known tunes with a strong, distinctive rhythm, like "Hail, Hail the Gang's All Here" or "Jingle Bells." As you get used to hearing rhythm separate from melody, you'll find that you can recognize tunes more easily.

At the beginning, it's a good idea to take turns tapping out the songs. After you play for a while, you can start following the standard rules:

One player taps out a tune. The player that guesses it becomes the tapper. If no one guesses the tune correctly, the original tapper gets another turn and taps out a new tune.

If just two of you are playing, take turns tapping, but a wrong guess gets you a point. Five points and you lose.

Twenty Questions

Players: 2 or more
Equipment: None
Preparation: None

"Twenty Questions" is a far better game than most people realize, or it can be if you use imagination when you choose your subject. It is one of the simplest guessing games, and people of all ages can play it.

One person thinks of a person, place or thing and announces to the group whether it is animal, vegetable or mineral.

Animal is anything from a human being to a sponge in the animal kingdom, but it can also be anything made from an animal skin (like a leather wallet) or it can be part of an animal, like the great white shark's jaws or a strip of bacon. It can also be groups of people—like all the people who live in

downtown Burbank or all the people who go out on blind dates. It can be supernatural creatures, like

Batman or Frankenstein, or nursery rhyme characters like Mary, Mary, Quite Contrary. It can also be part of a fictional person, like Dracula's tooth.

Vegetable is anything in the plant kingdom. It can be something that grows on trees or in the ground. It can be something made from things that grow—like paper or a book, like perfume or spaghetti. It can also be penicillin (made from bread mold), a rubber hot water bottle or skis—or some specific thing, like the Pines of Rome, the poison apple the Wicked Queen prepared for Snow White, or all the French fries that McDonald's serves in a year.

Mineral is just about everything else—rocks and stones, but also water, salt, glass, plastic or the Emerald City of Oz.

Back to the game: One player announces the classification of the subject and then the guessers get 20 questions in which to find out what it is. The questions must be ones that can be answered "Yes," "No," "Partly" or "Sometimes." The player who guesses what it is becomes the next player to select the subject.

Think out your questions very carefully so that you eliminate many possibilities each time. Questions that are too specific too soon can be a complete waste. If you think you know the answer and are not too near 20, continue to pin it down with general questions before you ask a direct one.

Here is a sample game (The subject is The Three Bears. Animal.):

1. Is it human? No.
2. Is it 4-legged? Yes.

3. Is this a carnivorous animal? No.
4. Is it bigger than a breadbox? (Few people have breadboxes these days, but this is a classic question.) Yes.
5. Is it bigger than I am? Partly. (The idea being that Pappa and Momma Bear are bigger, but Baby Bear isn't.)
6. Is more than one animal involved? Yes.
7. Are they land animals? Yes.
8. Are they dangerous? Yes.
9. Are they found in North America? Yes.
10. Are they hairy? Yes.
11. Are they bears? Yes.
12. Are they bears who attacked people? No.
13. Are these bears fictional? Yes.
14. Are there more than 3 of them? No.
15. Are they the Three Bears? Yes.

A few notes about strategy: If you find your friends often pick famous people as subjects, you might want to ask opening questions that identify them right away. When "Twenty Questions" was played on radio decades ago, the players used to ask, "Is this a living American male?" as a shortcut question. And it usually saved them lots of time! But whatever shortcut questions you develop will depend on your group. If you find that most of the subjects are film stars, you might want to ask, "Is this a living person in the entertainment world?" Of course, once people get used to your asking that kind of question, they'll start avoiding that category and reach further afield for subjects. But that will make the game more interesting, too.

You don't have to stick with individual people or

things as subjects. As you get skillful at this game, you may want to go really far out, with things like:

All the women in the world who are going to have twins

All the newlyweds at Niagara Falls

The heel of Cinderella's glass slipper

The tears on the faces of the girls that Georgie Porgie kissed

Who Are You?

Players: 2 or more
Equipment: None
Preparation: None

This is a simpler variation on "Twenty Questions," but it has a charm of its own. One of the players actually "becomes" the subject, and the others ask questions directly. Let's say that you have decided to be Clark Kent (Superman), and the game begins:

HARVEY: What is your profession?

YOU: I'm in journalism.

SANDY: Is that what made you famous?

YOU: Not really. I guess it was my work in law enforcement.

CASSIE: Are you married?

YOU: No.

CASSIE: In love?

YOU: Absolutely.

SANDY: What do you do for fun?

YOU: I don't have much time for fun, actually.

CASSIE: What keeps you so busy?

YOU: Well, I take my job very seriously. And a lot of people depend on me.

HARVEY: Are you American?

YOU: Yes—but I wasn't born in the States.

And so on. You can have some fun with the answers you give. While they have to be truthful, they don't have to be complete!

You're not limited to twenty questions in this game. The players just keep asking questions until they figure out who you are or give up. If they give up, you get to go again. The one who guesses your identity becomes the next mystery character.

This game can get more complex, too. Let's say that you're all the people who ever played hookey from school.

HARVEY: What is your profession?

YOU: I have many professions—I've done almost everything, in fact.

SANDY: What are you most famous for?

YOU: Well, I'm not exactly proud of that.

CAROL: Why is that?

YOU: It was something I wasn't supposed to do.

HARVEY: Something illegal?

YOU: Sort of.

CAROL: Did you profit from doing it?

YOU: I'm afraid not, but I thought I did at the time.

Sooner or later the others will realize that there is more than one of you, and gear all their questions to the thing you did and when you did it.

Grandma Is Strange

Players: 2 or more
Equipment: None
Preparation: None

In this game, each player takes turns having a strange grandmother. The first player—say, Laurie—starts out:

"My grandma is very strange. She loves tennis but she hates games."

Laurie's statement is based on a secret combination that she has thought up.

The next player asks a question, testing:

"Does she like carrots?"

"Yes," says Laurie, and gives them another clue, "but she hates peas."

"Does she like dogs?"

"No, but she's crazy about raccoons."

Laurie's secret combination is that her grandmother likes anything that has a double letter in it, like buttons—but not bows; zoos—but not animals; pepper—but not salt.

As players discover Laurie's grandmother's secret, they join her in giving clues to the other players.

You can go on for hours with this game. The last player to "catch on" to the secret is the next one to have a strange grandmother.

That's the usual way to play this game, and once you discover the formula, the game is over. But actually, this is where the fun begins. Grandma can be strange in different ways: she can hate anything that has a certain letter in it. Or anything that grows (watch out, that's a tricky one—*many* things grow). Or anything with two syllables (she hates flying but she loves jets). Or anything with two legs. Or 4-letter words. Or anything that doesn't smell.

Coffeepot

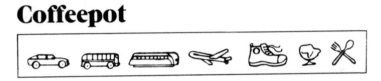

Players: **2–12**
Equipment: **None**
Preparation: **None**

In this game "Coffeepot" becomes a verb—a verb that you (or your group) think up secretly and that your opponent must guess by asking a series of questions. In each question the word "Coffeepot" is used for the hidden verb, and the questions must be answerable by "yes" or "no."

Suppose you are on the guessing end of the game. You might start with, "Do people Coffeepot?"

"Do I Coffeepot?"

"Do you Coffeepot?"

"Do all human beings Coffeepot?"

If the answer to the last question is no, you will need to narrow down the field and find out if only boys Coffeepot or perhaps only old people or only married women, etc. After you find out, or if you don't seem to be getting any results, try another tack: Do you need any tools to Coffeepot? Do you Coffeepot only in certain places or at certain times of the year or of the day? Do animals Coffeepot? Is Coffeepotting fun? Difficult? Part of a job? A natural function?

After you have narrowed down the field and think you are pretty sure you know what "Coffeepot" is, you get three guesses. It's a good idea, though, to ask as many specific questions as possible before you guess.

Suppose you've found out that young people Coffeepot but not small children; that you Coffeepot outdoors; that you don't Coffeepot in the dark; that you Coffeepot in warm weather; that you use a long pole to Coffeepot; that neither you nor your opponent Coffeepot yourselves; and that Coffeepotting takes skill, strength and practice. You think the answer may be "to pole vault." Then you might check to make sure by asking, "Do you need a very high hurdle to Coffeepot?" If the answer is yes, you know that you are right.

Too old to Coffeepot?

Too young?

If you're playing Coffeepot in a place where one person can leave the room, the others should decide what Coffeepot is. Then the guesser comes back in and asks each player one or more questions. When the guesser gets the answer, he or she selects the next one to guess.

If you're in close quarters in a car or in a restaurant, say, and more than two want to play, let one person select the Coffeepot word, while the others ask the questions.

Botticelli

Players: 2–10
Equipment: None
Preparation: None

Botticelli (pronounced Bah-ti-*CHELL*-ee) is one of the great guessing games, and it can be played by anyone from eight up. The more knowledgeable the group, the more fun the game.

One player thinks of a person, real or fictional, living or dead, and tells the group only the first letter of the person's last name. The others have to guess who it is, but they are only allowed to guess if they already have someone in mind. For instance, let's say the subject is Botticelli, the Italian artist. Here is part of a game:

MARK: I am a famous person whose name begins with B.

HAL: Are you a famous composer? (*He is thinking of Beethoven.*)

MARK: No, I am not Bach.

LIZ: Are you a character from the comics?

MARK: No, I am not Charlie Brown.

LAEL: Are you a comedy writer?

MARK: No, I am not Mel Brooks.

JIM: Are you an actor?

MARK: No, I am not George Burns.

HAL (*Still trying for Beethoven but he can't ask the same question the same way twice*): Are you a composer who went deaf?

MARK: No, I am not Beethoven.

(*HAL revealed too much. It would have been better if he had known some obscure fact about Beethoven that would disguise his idea so that MARK would not have thought of Beethoven so easily.*)

LIZ: Are you a U.S. President?

MARK (*stumped*): I challenge you.

LIZ: Buchanan!

(*LIZ, having stumped MARK, gets a leading question, which will help the group find out who MARK is. The leading question must be one that can be answered "yes" or "no."*)

LIZ: Are you male?

MARK: (*must answer a leading question truthfully*): Yes.

LAEL: Are you a famous painter? (*She is thinking of Botticelli.*)

MARK: Yes, but I am not Bosch.

(*MARK had to admit that LAEL had guessed the right category. But he didn't have to admit that he was Botticelli as long as he could think of another painter beginning with B.*)

JIM: Are you a famous general?

MARK (*stumped again*): I challenge you.

JIM: Napoleon Bonaparte! I get a leading question. Are you alive?

MARK: No.

HAL: Are you a famous baseball player?

MARK: No, I am not Yogi Berra.

LIZ: Are you a pioneer?

MARK: No, I am not Daniel Boone.

LAEL (*Still trying for Botticelli*): Are you a famous Italian painter?

MARK: Yes, but I am not Michelangelo Buonarroti.

(*Now* LAEL *is stumped. She doesn't know any more facts about Botticelli that she can use to ask another question. She cannot repeat her last question without changing it a little. She has to wait for a chance at a leading question before she can pinpoint the person. If she gets to stump* MARK *again, before anyone else does, she can ask if he is Botticelli, and then she will be the next one to think of a person.*)

BOTTICELLI FOR EXPERTS

For a much more difficult game, the players restrict their questions each time they get information through leading questions.

For example, once the players know that the subject is male, they can ask questions about only male subjects. Once they know, from a leading question, that the person is dead, they can ask questions only about dead people. Don't try this unless you're really a super-Botticelli player!

2
On the Road

You can play many of the games in other sections when you're in the car or on a bus, but some games have been invented especially for motor trips. They don't get you involved in words or ideas (at least, most of them don't), but they're focused primarily on the road: the other cars, the license plates, the countryside, the signs.

And because few family motor trips would be complete without singing at least one or two songs, we've also included a handful of the best-loved songs for singing in the car, with a bunch of verses to get you going.

The Bus Stop Game

Players: 2
Equipment: None
Preparation: None

Just because the name of this game is so exact, there's no reason to limit it to bus stops. It's a good game to play any time you're waiting near a two-way street or highway.

You score one point for every car that passes from the right. Your friend scores one for every car that passes from the left. When your wait is over (the bus comes, the driver gets back, your friend arrives—whatever), the one with the most points wins.

Collecting Cars

Players: 2 or more
Equipment: Paper and pencil (optional)
Preparation: None

The object of the game is to "collect" as many cars as you can. You collect a car by "owning" the place it comes from—or some other fact you can get from the license plate. If you're in the U.S. or Australia, for example, you own the state. And you get to own a state by being the first person to spot a car from that state. Let's say that you're in Connecticut, and you just started out on your trip. Cars from Connecticut, New York and New Jersey are automatically out of the game—because there are just too many of them. But you're the first to spot a car from Louisiana.

"Louisiana!" you shout, "I own Louisiana!" And for the rest of the game, any time you see a car from Louisiana, it gets added to your score: one point per car.

If you're walking or driving in Canada, you can play the game by owning the different provinces (NOT the one you're in). If you're travelling in the U.K., you can play it by owning one of the letters or digits on the marker (the license plate). All cars with a 6 on the marker, for instance, could be owned, and so could all cars with an L or all cars with a combination of 6 and M.

One of the passengers or walkers can keep tabs on who owns which state, province, digit, letter or combination—in case there's a dispute—but usually everyone remembers. You can decide ahead of time how long you want to play—or play until you arrive at your destination. The one with the most points wins.

License Plate Numbers

Players:	1 or more
Equipment:	A watch (optional)
Preparation:	None

This is a good game to play in heavy traffic, especially

when a lot of cars are passing you. The object is to find numbers from 1–20 on the license plates you see along the road. The rule is that you can score only one number at a time in sequence.

For example, let's say the first license plate you see is NSW 5. You can't score any points because the only number you can use at this point in the game is a 1. If a car came along with the license plate 1M237, for instance, you'd be able to score the number 1, and then you'd need to start looking for a license plate with a 2 in it. You can't score the 2 and 3 from the same plate, because only one number can be scored from any one license plate. When you get into double numbers—from 10 to 20—the two digits you need must come side by side. S7FU208, for example, would give you 20, but S7FU028 wouldn't.

If you're playing alone, take a look at your watch before you start and see how long it takes you to locate all 20 numbers. Then you can play against your best time.

If you're playing with more than one person, the first one to spot the needed number is the one who gets to score. And each player works on his or her own count. So that one person can be looking for an 18 while another is searching for an 8.

This game can get exciting for the players. But don't ask the driver to play! That can get hair-raising!

LICENSE PLATE NUMBERS—THE FAST GAME

Use the same rules as before, but this time allow more than one number to score from any license plate. For example, the license plate 123M7 would give you 1 and 2 and 3, and if any players were up to 12 in their lists, they could claim that number in the same turn.

License Plate Letters

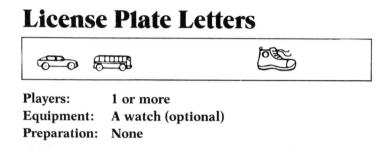

Players: 1 or more
Equipment: A watch (optional)
Preparation: None

This game is played the same way, but instead of the numbers 1–20, you search for the letters A to Z.

License Plate Words

Players: 1 or more
Equipment: None
Preparation: None

This license plate game goes one step further than finding numbers or letters. Here the players select words, phrases or even sentences that they are going to try to spell out from license plates.

In any one round, every player needs to pick a word or phrase with exactly the same number of letters. The length depends on how long you want the game to last. Anywhere from six to ten letters makes a good game. Starting with six letters, for example, you could use:

BE COOL

BIG MAC

BY JOVE

CATNIP

GO HOME

HOT DOG

OLD HAT

SLY FOX

or anything else with six letters. After each player picks a word, phrase or sentence, you race to see who can spell it out first from the letters on the license plates of passing cars. You can take a letter from anywhere in the license plate: so A875BQ and BI67WA and CAT95 would all give you an A, but you can't take a letter from a license plate if someone else claimed the letter first.

If Barry's phrase is COLD CASH, for instance, he can take the C from CAT 95 if he claims it first, and then no one else can use it for a different phrase. But Julia, if her phrase is AWAY WE GO, can take the A from the same license plate (CAT95). And another player can take the T.

You need to collect all the letters in the right order. So if MAKE MY DAY is your phrase, you need to find an M first, then an A, then a K and so on. Decide beforehand whether one player may take two or more letters from the same license plate. For example, could a player with the word CATNIP take the CAT from the CAT95 license plate? It's up to you—but if you allow it the game goes faster.

Here are a few more ideas for words and phrases:

With 7 letters:
ALL OF ME
BAD SHOT
BIG BIRD
DOWN BOY
DRACULA
GOOD DOG
HALFWIT
OLD MAID
RAT FINK

Napoleon

With 8 letters:
AWAY WE GO
CALM DOWN
CRAZY MAN
GO TO JAIL
I LOVE YOU
LUCKY DAY
NAPOLEON
STARSHIP

Good dog

With 9 letters:
BOARDWALK
BROAD JUMP
GOING NUTS
HAPPY DAYS
MAKE MY DAY
PARK PLACE
ROCKY ROAD
SAY CHEESE

With 10 letters:
ADAM AND EVE
CINDERELLA
DONALD DUCK
FLINTSTONE
GO FOR BROKE
HAVE A HAPPY
NEW ENGLAND
RUB A DUB DUB

If you're playing alone, as in the other license plate games, you can time yourself and play against your best score.

Number of the Day

Players: 1 or more
Equipment: A watch (optional)
Preparation: None

The players decide on an order of play—clockwise or counterclockwise—in the car or bus or whatever. And then they pick a number: let's say, number 5.

The first car to pass belongs to Tom, the first player. The license plate is 867EN. No 5's. Tom's turn is over.

The second player, Dick, gets the next car to pass: 151N81. He scores one point for the 5.

Now it's Harry's turn. The next car to come along has the license plate 55CN25. Harry gets 3 points—one for each of the 5's.

And it's Tom's turn again.

First player to get 25 points wins. If you want a short game, set a lower winning number.

If you want to play the game alone, time yourself to see how long it takes you to get to your goal number. Then play against your own best time.

Car of Your Choice

Players: 2 or more
Equipment: A watch
Preparation: None

Each player chooses a make of car: Toyota, Ford, Chevrolet, or whatever. Over a set period of time, say 15 minutes, each one tries to spot as many models from that car maker as possible. When the time is up, the player who spotted the most cars is the winner.

Alphabet on Road and Track

Players: 2 or more
Equipment: Paper and pencil for each player or team
Preparation: None

Contestants may be two individuals or two teams. Each of you looks for the first sign you can find—a billboard or a road sign—that contains an A—such as, "Downtown Augusta—turn right."

The player (or the team) that sees it first writes it down and circles the A.

Then you try to find a road sign containing a B. The first player (or team) to complete the alphabet wins. If you spot a phrase containing two desired letters *in order*, such as the D and E in DovEr, you may copy that word and circle both letters.

Eagle Eye

Players: **2 or more**
Equipment: **A list you draw up ahead of time**
Preparation: **See below.**

To begin the game, draw up a list of the objects you are likely to see as you drive along, taking into consideration the kind of road you're on and the part of the country you're in. For example, you would assign a higher point value to an Eskimo if you happen to be in Brazil than you would while driving through Alaska. The player who sights the object first gets the points, and every time the same sort of object is sighted again, you can score it again.

Winner is the player who gets the highest score in a given period of time, usually half an hour.

Here is a sample scale of points:

Rest stop 1
Horses (one, a pair a herd) 2
Red light 1
Railroad crossing 2
Freight train 2
Red barn 1
Farmer in field 2
Farmer in field with plow 4
Cyclist 3
Sheep (one, a pair or herd) 2
Fast-food restaurant 1
Golfer 4
Lightning rod 2
Lake, pond or river 1
Motorboat or rowboat 2
Fisherman 3
Pheasant, duck or turkey 4
Hay wagon 5
Deer 6
Cows (one, a pair, or herd) 2

Car Lotto

Players: 2–5
Equipment: A score card for each player,
prepared as described below
A pencil for each player
Preparation: Make each score card into a lotto
card that looks like this:

or like this:

Fill in each box with the name of a
different person or thing in the
desired category. Each card should
be somewhat different. You can use
the individual items on more than
one card, but put them in a
different order.

This game takes a bit of preparation, but it's worth it.
The idea is that you set up your own lotto cards before
the trip starts, with special items on them that you'll
encounter as you drive along. For instance, you could
fill in the boxes with some of the items in the Eagle
Eye list (pages 32–33) that you're likely to see as you
drive. Or you could fill the boxes with the names of
the singers you're likely to hear on the car radio.

One card might look like this:

Billy Joel	The Beatles	Peter, Paul & Mary
Bruce Spring-steen	Frank Sinatra	Madonna
Whitney Houston	Stevie Wonder	Elton John

Another might look like this:

Frank Sinatra	Simon & Garfunkel	The Beach Boys
Madonna	Billy Joel	Ella Fitzgerald
The Beatles	Olivia Newton-John	Michael Jackson

Then, when you're ready to start, turn on the radio. As each singer comes on, the players with that performer on their cards cross the name out. The first player to cross out a name in every box in a row—horizontally, vertically or diagonally—wins.

It's a good idea for one person to keep track of all

the performers as their numbers are played, so that disputes can be settled easily.

This game will work with other categories, too. You can play it with musical groups, individual musicians, commercials, subjects on the news, makes of cars, popular songs, and famous people whose names are mentioned on the news.

Here are a few sample cards:

Pope John	Ronald Reagan	Gorbachev
Margaret Thatcher	Qadafi	Ayatollah Khomeini
Oral Roberts	Edward Kennedy	Elizabeth Taylor

Famous people in the news

Commercials

Bank	Food	Beverage
Restaurant	Clothing Store	Beauty Product
Auto	Station Promotion	Health Product

Flash Categories

Players:	**2–6**
Equipment:	**A dozen or more small cards or sturdy paper cut down to business card size**
Preparation:	**On each card write the name of a classification, such as Flower, Gem, Month, State, Country, Article of Clothing, Television Program, Color, Opera, Playwright, Composer, Artist, etc.**

Shuffle the cards and place the pack face down. The player who goes first calls out a letter of the alphabet, turns up the top card and reads it aloud. Then each player tries to name something in the category that starts with the letter that was called. The first one to think of an object in that category gets the card. It might go like this:

KRISTIN: G. (*Turning up the top card*) Monster.

NEAL: Godzilla. (*KRISTIN gives him the card and the pack. It is now NEAL's turn. He takes a card from the top of the pack.*) Cartoon character.

ERIC: Gilligan. (*He takes the card from NEAL, and the pack. Removing the top card from the pack*) Hero. (*No one can think of a hero beginning with G, so the card goes back to the bottom of the pack and ERIC takes another card from the top. But this time, he changes the letter.*) S (*Reads top card*) Actor.

NEAL: George C. Scott.

And so on. Play the game until all the cards are won (if possible) and the player with the greatest number of cards wins.

Keep the cards in the glove compartment. You can use them over and over to play "Flash Categories."

Night Rider

Players: **2 or more**
Equipment: **None**
Preparation: **None**

There are plenty of car games to play by day when there's a great deal to look at, but when it's night and you're on a dull road—and feeling a little dull yourself—what do you play? "Night Rider," of course! It's a different kind of game, because nobody wins. Nobody can. All you have to do is make a sound—a different sound—whenever a particular situation comes up.

When a car passes you, for example, everyone says BZZZ, BZZZ, BZZZ. When you pass another car, everyone says EEEE, EEEE, EEEE.

Here are a few of the most common "events" and the sounds that go with them:

> **Car passes:** BZZZ, BZZZ, BZZZ
> **You pass car:** EEEE, EEEE, EEEE
> **You go over bridge:** OOOO, OOOO, OOOO
> **You go under bridge (or underpass):** AYE,
>   AYE, AYE

You pass sign: AHHH, AHHH, AHHH
You pass truck: WHEE, WHEE, WHEE
Truck passes you: WOOF, WOOF, WOOF

As you get used to playing the game, you'll want to make up other sounds to go with other happenings. Different types of signs could call for different responses. Trailers, cars pulling boats, and motorcycles could each get sounds of their own. And the players take turns choosing what sound goes with that.

Silly game? You bet. Especially when three or four of these events take place at the same time. You're going over a bridge, say, and there's a sign saying Exit 16, and a truck passes you, and it comes out:

OOOO, OOOO, OOOO, AHHH, AHHH, AHHH, WOOF, WOOF, WOOF all the way across!

The more people who play this game the better. And the noisier.

Of course, after you play this game a few times, you may find yourself barking every time a truck passes you in heavy traffic—and that could be a bit difficult to explain—but that's one of the risks you take. . . .

Travel Songs

Players: 2 or more
Equipment: None
Preparation: None

The great songs for travelling fall into a few different categories. First there are the songs that are sung ONLY when you're travelling, such as:

We're Here (to the tune of "Auld Lang Syne")

We're here, because we're here,
Because we're here, because we're here.
We're here, because we're here,
Because we're here, because we're here. . . .

and so on, forever, until you get there.

Or the famous walking song:

99 Miles

Oh, I'm 99 miles from home,
I'm 99 miles from home,
I walk a while and rest a while,
I'm 99 miles from home. . . .

and then, "I'm 98 miles from home. . . ." and so on
until you get there—or until you can't stand it anymore.

And another song that repeats and repeats:

Around the Corner

Around the corner and under the tree—
A sergeant major, once said to me,
"Who would marry you?" I would like to know,
For every time I look at your face,
It makes me want to go—around the corner. . . .

and so on and on and on and on.

Or the famous end-of-vacation song:

Ten More Days

Ten more days of vacation,
Then we go back to the station,
Back to civilization—
We don't want to go home!
We don't want to go home—
We don't want to go home—
We want to stay right here.

Then you sing "Nine more days of vacation" and then
"Eight more" until you come to the end:

No more days of vacation,
Now we go to the station,
Back to civilization—
Now we have to go home!

There are also the many-verse songs for marching, such as:

The Ants Go Marching

The ants go marching one by one, hurrah, hurrah,
The ants go marching one by one, hurrah, hurrah,
The ants go marching one by one
The little one stops to suck his thumb
And they all go marching out in the big parade.

Then the ants go marching:

2×2: **The little one stops to tie his shoe.**

3×3: **The little one stops to climb a tree**

4×4: **The little one stops to sleep some more**

5×5: **The little one stops to joke and jive**

6×6: **The little one stops to do some tricks**

7×7: **The little one stops to point to heaven**

8×8: **The little one stops to shut the gate**

9×9: **The little one stops to read a sign**

10×10: **The little one stops to say THE END (*and stop singing*).**

And then there are songs for which you contribute your own verse while everyone else sings the chorus, such as "You Can't Get to Heaven." If the people on the bus or in the car are terrifically creative, they might want to come up with their own new verses. Otherwise, here are a huge number of verses to keep you going for miles!

You Can't Get to Heaven

Oh, you can't get to heaven
On roller skates
Cause you'll roll right by
Those pearly gates.

Oh, you can't get to heaven
In a rocking chair
Cause the rocking chair
Won't take you there.

Oh, you can't get to heaven
In a trolley car
Cause the gosh darn thing
Won't go that far.

Oh, you can't get to heaven
On a rocket ship
Cause the rocket ship
Won't make the trip.

Oh, you can't get to heaven
In a limousine,
Cause the Lord don't sell
No gasoline.

Oh, you can't get to heaven
With fear and doubt
Cause the Lord wants you
To cast them out.

Oh, you can't get to heaven
On a pizza pie,
Cause the pizza pie
Won't fly that high.

Oh, you can't get to heaven
With chocolate chips
Cause the Lord don't like
Them on your hips.

Oh, you can't get to heaven
On brand new wheels
Cause the Lord won't make
No discount deals.

Oh, you can't get to heaven
With powder and paint
Cause the Lord don't like
You as you ain't.

Oh, you can't get to heaven
On a pair of skis
Cause you'll schuss through
St. Peter's knees.

Oh, you can't get to heaven
With Superman
Cause the Lord he is
A Batman fan.

If you get to heaven
Before I do
Just bore a hole
And pull me through.

If I get to heaven
Before you do
I'll plug that hole
With shavings and glue.

That's all there is
There ain't no more
St. Peter said,
And closed the door.

How about the elimination songs like "Bingo," in
which you leave out another letter every time you
sing, and just clap instead. The fun is in the sounds
you DON'T sing together:

Bingo

There was a farmer had a dog
And Bingo was his name, oh!
B-I-N-G-O B-I-N-G-O B-I-N-G-O
And Bingo was his name, oh.

There was a farmer had a dog
And Bingo was his name, oh!
(*Clap*) I-N-G-O (*Clap*) I-N-G-O (*Clap*) I-N-G-O
And Bingo was his name, oh.

And so on until you sing:

There was a farmer had a dog
And Bingo was his name, oh!
(*Clap, clap, clap, clap, clap—clap, clap, clap, clap,
clap—Clap, clap, clap, clap, clap*)
And Bingo was his name, oh!

Don't forget the great rounds that sound so marvelous as you sing them together. It's important though that everyone knows them *very well* so each one can hold the melody and isn't sidetracked by other—maybe stronger—singers. For that reason, the most well known songs are the winners. Try them.

Merrily We Roll Along

Merrily we roll along
Roll along, roll along
Merrily we roll along
O'er the deep blue sea.

Row, Row, Row Your Boat

Row, row, row your boat
Gently down the stream,
Merrily, merrily, merrily, merrily
Life is but a dream.

Frere Jacques

Frere Jacques, Frere Jacques
Dormez-vous? Dormez vous?
Sonnez les matines, sonnez les matines,
Ding, dong, ding, ding dong ding.

Three Blind Mice

Three blind mice, three blind mice,
See how they run, see how they run.
They all ran after the farmer's wife,
She cut off their tails with a carving knife
Did you ever see such a sight in your life—
As three blind mice.

And there are hundreds of other songs that help make
long trips shorter. Singing is probably the best entertainment of all for motor trips, and it's wonderful in
most other situations as well. Few things make you
feel better. Try your own favorites.

3
Wonderful Word Games

Some of the games in this section are classic games you've been playing for years, but it just wouldn't be right to leave them out of a book of the best games to play when you're travelling—or sitting—and exercising your mental muscles. Most of the games have some depth to them. You can play them in a lazy way, with half your mind, and enjoy them all right—or you can use your wits and come up with a vividly colorful world of word play. Take your pick!

Ghost and Double Ghost

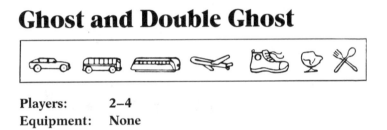

Players:	2–4
Equipment:	None
Preparation:	None

"Ghost" is a game of word building. The first player says a letter—any letter—that begins a word and the next player adds a letter to it. The object of the game is to force one of the other players to complete a word by the addition of his or her letter, and avoid forming a complete word yourself. Three-letter words don't count.

The player who ends the word gets the "G" of the word *Ghost*. The second miss makes for an H, the third an O. Whoever becomes a G-H-O-S-T first loses.

You must have a word in mind when you add a letter to the word-in-process. If the next player can't think of a word that can be formed from the letters already given, you may be challenged. Then, if you can produce a word, it counts as a miss for the player who challenged you. If you are bluffing, with no real word in mind, you lose and become a fifth more of a ghost than you were before.

That's plain "Ghost." In "Double Ghost" the first player starts by giving two letters. Then the next player can add one letter either at the beginning or at the end.

Here is a sample game:

JOE: RT.

FLO: ORT.

JOE: ORT-H.

FLO (*She doesn't want to make it "north," but "northerly" is a word*): ORTH-E.

JOE: ORTHE-R.

FLO (*Suddenly realizing that "northerly" ends on her, but that "northern" will end on* JOE): ORTHER-N.

JOE (*hoping that* FLO *will not think of the word "northernmost," and will challenge him*): ORTHERN-M.

And the game continues until NORTHERNMOST is reached and Joe becomes a G of a ghost.

SUPER-GHOST

Only for people with wonderful vocabularies: try playing "Double Ghost," starting with two letters and adding two letters each time!

Word Strings

Players: **2 or more**
Equipment: **None**
Preparation: **None**

You play this game in the same way you play "Ghost," but you don't have to stop once you complete a word—*if* you can come up with a letter that builds the word further. The object of the game is to keep adding letters until the word can no longer be increased.

Example:
ANNE: H.

BILL: A.

CATHY: P.

DANA: P.

ANNE: E.

BILL: N. (*BILL would now be a G in an ordinary game of "Ghost," but in this game, CATHY is the one who would get the G if she couldn't continue the word. But she can.*)

CATHY: S.

   (*Will he do it?*)

DANA : T.

   (*He did it.*)

ANNE: A.

BILL: N.

CATHY: C.

DANA: E.

ANNE (*Can't think of any way to continue the word*): Okay, I'm a G.

I Love My Love with an A

Players: **2 or more**
Equipment: **None**
Preparation: **None**

Remember "A My Name Is Alice?" Well, this is a more complex version of it.

> The first player starts:
> "I love my love with an A because he is *adventurous*.
> I loathe my love with an A because he is *annoying*.
> His name is *Albert*. He lives in *Australia* and he *adores ants* that he feeds on *antipasto*."

It's a little more complicated than "A My Name Is," but it doesn't have any different principles involved in it. Instead of filling in four blanks (A my name is *Alice* and my husband's name is *Albert*. We live in *Australia* and we sell *apples*), you fill in six slightly more demanding ones:

- 2 adjectives (*adventurous* and *annoying*), which can be fun
- the usual name of the lover and place (*Albert* and *Australia*)
- a silly hobby or occupation (*adoring ants*)
- a silly activity (feeding them *antipasto*)

Second player continues with B:

> "I love my love with a B because he is *bold*.
> I loathe my love with a B because he is *boring*.

His name is *Bart*. He lives in *Burbank* and he *beats bears* after he takes them *bowling*."

That's all there is to it. On with letter C. A ridiculous game? Absolutely! But it's fun.

Dance Daringly in Denmark

Players: **2 or more**
Equipment: **None**
Preparation: **None**

"A My Name is Alice" has endless variations. Here's another complex version that has some style.

The first player starts with A, saying, "I'm taking a trip to A——— (Afghanistan, for example). What will I do there?"

The next player must answer with a verb and

another word beginning with the same letter as the name of the place.

"Act arrogant," would be a possible answer.

Then the second player poses the B question: "I'm taking a trip to Barcelona," for example. "What will I do there?"

Player #3 might answer "Bake biscuits in Barcelona," and then throw a C to Player #4, who may recommend chewing cookies in Canberra, and so on.

The game goes through the alphabet. If players can't come up with a question or an answer within a reasonable time, they get one count against them. Three counts and they're out of the game. Winner is the last one left.

Snip!

Players:	2 or more
Equipment:	None
Preparation:	None

Traditionally, "Snip!" is played with a knotted handkerchief. The one who is "It" starts the game by throwing the hanky to one of the other players. But you don't need a handkerchief. "It" can just point, or if only two are playing they can take turns.

In any case, as you ("It") toss the handkerchief (but before you point), call out a word of three letters. Then, as soon as the handkerchief is caught by one of the players—or immediately after you point—start counting to 12.

The player who got the handkerchief (or is pointed at), must respond with three words that begin with any of the letters in the word you called out. And the player must do it before you can finish counting. Because when you get to 12 and yell "Snip!" the player is out.

For example, let's say you call out the word "Man" and point a finger at David. He has to use letters M A and N. He could shout, "Make a Nightgown," or "Mean and Nutty," or just three unrelated words, such as "Meat, Animals, Neckties."

But whatever David replies, he has to get out the last word before you finish counting to 12. If David does it successfully, he becomes "It."

If you want to make the game more difficult, you can decide beforehand that every player must come up with related words—or even a full sentence. But more players will get snipped that way, which might make the game fairly short.

If only two are playing, let every snip count one point in favor of the snipper. Three snips win.

Geography Games

Players: 2 or more
Equipment: None
Preparation: None

This is an ideal game to play on a motor trip—especially if you're the one holding the map!

In basic Geography, the person who starts the game gives the name of a city or state or country or island or body of water or mountain. It is up to the next person to name another place—one whose name begins with the same letter that the first place ended with.

Here is a sample game:

CYD: Brisbane.

ROBERT: England.

BARBARA: Denmark.

CARLOS: Kentucky.

JEAN: York.

LISA: Kansas.

CYD: Suva.

ROBERT: Atlanta.

BARBARA: Australia.

When a player can't think of a place that begins with the right letter, that player is out. The game continues until there is just one person left in it, the winner.

Words like "Islands," "Rivers" and "Mountains" are not allowed. You wouldn't say "The Philippine Islands," for example, but "The Philippines." You wouldn't say "Nile River," but "The Nile"—(and words like "the" or "an" don't count). You wouldn't say "Mount Everest," but just, "Everest." No plurals are permitted either: The Finger Lakes, for instance, would be eligible only individually.

No place name may be said more than once. Since, after the game has been going for a while, some players take very long (and boring) amounts of time to come up with a name, it is a good idea to set a time limit for each player. The shorter the time limit, the more interesting the game.

Hint: One of the problems with the game is that once you get started naming places beginning with A, it seems that most of them end with A, too, and the game can get bogged down. Here are some A's that don't end in A, to use when you need them:

Aberdeen	The Aleutians	Andes	Armidale
Abilene	Algiers	Andover	Arnhem
Abingdon	Alice Springs	Annapolis	the Arno
Acapulco	Allentown	Ann Arbor	Asheville
Adelaide	Alsace	Antibes	Assisi
Adrian	Amalfi	Antioch	Athens
Afghanistan	Amarillo	Antwerp	Atlantic City
Aiken	Amazon	Anzio	the Atlantic
Alamo	Ames	Appalachians	Auburn
Albany	Amherst	Arctic Circle	Austin
Albion	Amsterdam	the Arctic	Avignon
Albuquerque	Anaheim	Arezzo	the Avon
Alderney	Anchorage	Arkansas	Ayers Rock
Aldershot	Anderson	Armentieres	the Azores

There also seems to be a shortage of E's, because so many place names end with them. Here are a few to remember:

Easter Island	Elizabeth	Englewood	Euclid
Easthampton	Elkton	Enid	Eureka
East Lynn	Ellendale	Enterprise	Europe
Easton	Ellsworth	Erie	Euston
Ecuador	Elmhurst	Erin	Evanston
Eden	Elmira	Erskine	Evansville
Edinburgh	Elmwood	Escondido	Everett
Edmond	El Paso	Essen	Everglades
Edmondton	El Salvador	Essex	Evergreen
Egypt	Encino	Estonia	Excelsior
Elba	Endicott	Ethiopia	Exeter
Eldorado	Enfield	Etna	Exmoor
Elgin	England	Eton	Eyre

Other End-Games

You can play "Geography" with any other subject your group is interested in. If you're into theatre, you can do it with plays or movies. The only problem is that so many titles end in E that you quickly run out of E's. It makes the game more interesting if you either outlaw any title that ends with E, after a certain point in the game, or agree to use the next-to-last letter when E titles run out.

You can play it with songs if you're into music, with characters in books, with athletes' names, or names of movie stars. Make up your own rules to ease your way over the rough spots (like the A and E problems).

The Missing Letter

Players: 2 or more
Equipment: None
Preparation: None

This game seems simple, but it's deceptive.

All you have to do is ask the other player a question and then mention a single letter of the alphabet. Your opponent must answer your question with a sentence which does not use that letter at all! Answers may be serious or silly. Then it is the next player's turn to answer a question, leaving out a specified letter. Simple? Wait till you try to express yourself without the letter E or the letter S! Writing instead of speaking makes it easier—but not much!

Here are some sample questions and answers:

What did you learn in school today? S.
I can't remember anything.

What did you do last summer? E.
Nothing much. . . . It was dark.

What do you put in your pen to write with? I.
We use pea soup.

What do you live in? H.
I live in a large zoo.

Hinky Pinky

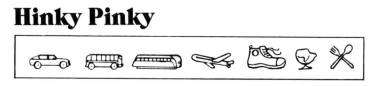

Players:	2 or more
Equipment:	None
Preparation:	None

You can play "Hinky Pinky" anywhere and any time—even by mail! A Hinky Pinky is a phrase made up of two 2-syllable rhyming words, such as "Silly filly."

In order to play, all you have to do is define your Hinky Pinky, and the other player must guess what it is. For example, you might say, "I have a Hinky Pinky meaning an unpleasant part of the face." The other players would have to guess the answer. In this case, it's a "horrid forehead."

Here are a few Hinky Pinkies. Can you figure them out? Answers on page 128.

1. Fowl that wins the lottery
2. Powerful sleepwear
3. Revolting couple
4. Hamlet's mother
5. A less healthy heart
6. A wicked insect
7. Small space vehicle
8. A fat ape
9. A hen who works in a chorus line
10. A scribble made by a piece of pasta

If you want to add to the game, you can try Hink Pinks and Hinkity Pinkities, too. A Hink Pink is a shorter

Hinky Pinky. It's made up of two one-syllable words, such as "Fat cat."

Here are some Hink Pinks:

1. An enormous boat
2. An ape who overeats compulsively
3. A hen that has a bad cold
4. What rodents have when they get together to talk
5. A vulgar thoroughbred
6. A sad buddy
7. When your boat sinks in the middle of a huge lake, what do you have?
8. A vegetable that has really put it all together
9. A sneaky insect
10. A bird who's not very bright

Hinkity Pinkities are rare. Here's one:
King Kong

And so are 4-syllable HPs. Try this:
Kojak couldn't hold onto a whirly bird.

It's as much fun to make up Hinky Pinkies as it is to guess them. Maybe more.

Answers on page 128.

4
Nutty Games

Many of the games in the previous chapters are funny, but the ones in this section have a special nuttiness to them. They're all different, all kind of silly, and all a lot of fun to play. In fact, part of the fun is seeing how silly they can get. And—sometimes—how confused the players can get. Have a ridiculous time with them!

Funny-Grams

Players:	6 or more
Equipment:	A sheet of paper or small pad for every player
	A pencil for every player
Preparation:	None

Fewer than six can play this game, but it's not as entertaining as with more players.

A leader reads a list of four or five letters of the alphabet. Each person is to write a message using these letters as the first letters of each word, in the order the letters are read.

Suppose the letters given are A, B, D and R. One

message might read, "A Bear Does Roar." Others might be, "Annie Bathes Daily, Remember?" or "Anxious Baboons Don't Rest."

After the players have finished making up their Funny-Grams, they take turns reading them out loud, and that's when the fun begins.

Note: After using easy letters to begin with, you can slip in some harder ones—Q, Y, J, etc., and the messages will get even sillier and funnier.

The Woollcott Game

Players:	2 or more
Equipment:	Pencil and paper
	A watch or clock—digital—or with
	a sweep second hand
Preparation:	None

Alexander Woollcott, the famous American author and critic, has been credited with inventing this one-minute game for two.

Your opponent keeps score and does the timing while you concentrate for 60 seconds. During that minute, you must think up all the words you can that start with a given letter. That's all there is to it!

Sounds easy, doesn't it? Well, try it. The timekeeper says, "Start when I give you the letter—R," and then starts timing. As you call off words that begin with R, the timekeeper keeps track of them by marking them off in groups of 5, like this: ⊬⊬

Of course, the dictionary is packed with common

words beginning with every letter of the alphabet, but you'll be surprised how difficult it is to think of them as you sit there faced by that relentless second hand, not to mention the grinning timekeeper!

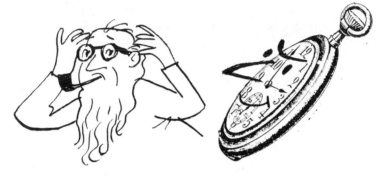

When the minute is up, total up the score and then change roles. Give each other letters of similar ease or difficulty (see below). If you get a Z, you're entitled to give a Y, but an S deserves a C.

Order of frequency as a starting letter: S-C-P-A-B-T-M-D-R-H-E-F-L-G-I-W-N-O-U-V-K-J-Q-Y-Z-X.

Backward Alphabet

Players: 2 or more
Equipment: Watch with a second-hand or a stop watch
Preparation: None

Each player in turn recites the alphabet backwards. The one who can do it fastest is the winner. The other players watch for omissions, and anyone skipping a letter is out.

Frozen Yogurt

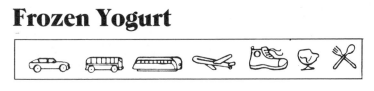

Players: 2 or more
Equipment: None
Preparation: None

You think of a noun and try to keep it secret while the other players try to guess what it is. They ask questions about anything they want. You answer all their questions any way you like—truthfully or untruthfully—but in every answer you have to mention the secret noun. How can you mention it and keep it secret at the same time? Because instead of actually saying the noun, you say, "Frozen yogurt."

For example, if the secret noun were "ghost," the game might go like this:

MICHELLE: How do you feel today?
YOU: Not as bad as a frozen yogurt.
SONJA: What is your favorite thing to do?
YOU: Tell frozen yogurt stories.
MARK: Where are you going for the holidays?
YOU: Out west to visit a frozen yogurt town.
JOHN: What's your favorite song?
YOU: "I Don't Stand a Frozen Yogurt of a Chance With You."
MICHELLE: What's your favorite movie?
YOU: Frozen Yogurt Busters.

The first player to guess what the frozen yogurt stands for gets a chance to choose the next subject. Any player who guesses incorrectly drops out. If nobody guesses, you get to choose another noun.

If frozen yogurt doesn't appeal to you, substitute something else—like pepperoni pizza, chocolate eclair, onion bagel or Diet Coke!

Your Monkey's Moustache

Players: 2
Equipment: None
Preparation: None

This game is similar to "Frozen Yogurt" because you keep saying a phrase over and over again in answer to questions, but it's a different type of game. The object here is to keep from laughing.

One person is "It." The others select a phrase that "It" must answer to every question. The group could

pick, "Your monkey's moustache," for example, or "six smelly sneakers," or "Harpo Marx," or "Uncle Andy's truss."

Then each person in the group gets to ask a question, such as, "What are you going to have for dinner tonight?" or "Who did you spend most of your time with last summer?" Of course, questions are tailored to be as hilarious as possible when answered by the phrase picked beforehand. And if "It" laughs, "It" is out. Winner is the biggest grouch.

Cheeseburger

Players: 2 or more
Equipment: None
Preparation: None

Have you ever played "Buzz"? It's a counting game, in which the players say the word "Buzz" whenever they come to the number 7 or a multiple or combination of it. Since that game was invented, many variations on it have appeared. The latest one was inspired by a skit from *Saturday Night Live*.

The players count off in a regular order. Player #1 says, "One." Player #2 says, "Two" and so on, until you get to number 7. Then instead of saying "Seven," or "Buzz," you say, "Cheeseburger" (pronounced "Chiz-bugga"). It goes like this:

1–2–3–4–5–6-
Cheeseburger-8–9–10–11–12–13-
Cheeseburger-15–16-Cheeseburger-18–19–20-

**Cheeseburger-22–23–24–25–26-
Cheeseburger-Cheeseburger-29–30–31–32–
33–34-Cheeseburger-36-Cheeseburger-38–
39–40–41-Cheeseburger-43–44–45–46-
Cheeseburger-48-Cheeseburger-50–51–52–
53–54–55-Cheeseburger-Cheeseburger-58–
59–60–61–62-Cheeseburger-64–65–66-
Cheeseburger-68–69-Cheeseburger -
Cheeseburger One-Cheeseburger Two-
Cheeseburger Three-Cheeseburger Four-
Cheeseburger Five-Cheeseburger Six-
Cheeseburger-Cheeseburger-Cheeseburger
Eight-Cheeseburger Nine-80, and so on, to 100.**

Anyone who hesitates, misses, or says "Seven" or any multiple of it, is OUT.

So far, it's just like Buzz. Now for more complications. Next time, keep on saying Cheeseburger for 7, but also say "Pepsi" for 5 and any multiple of it. It goes like this:

**1–2–3–4-Pepsi-6-Cheeseburger-8–9-
Pepsi-11–12–13-Cheeseburger-Pepsi, and so on.**

Thirty-five, which is both a multiple of 7 and 5, would be Cheeseburger-Pepsi, and so would 70.

CHEESEBURGER WITH FRIES

Ready for more? If you're still hanging in there after all that, you can add "Fries" for 3, so it would go like this:

**1–2-Fries-4-Pepsi-Fries-Cheeseburger-8-Fries-
Pepsi-11-Fries-Fries-Cheeseburger, and so on.**

It's practically impossible to do it with any kind of speed. This should put a riotous end to the game, no matter how skillful the players!

Thoughts

Players: 2 or more
Equipment: None
Preparation: None

You decide on a subject—some object, person or idea—and don't tell the others what it is. Then you ask the other players, one by one, what your thought is like. The players can answer anything they like. They could say your thought is like Johnny Carson, for example, or like a pickle or like a sick elephant.

Then you tell them what your thought is and ask each player to defend the answer that was given.

For instance, you would say, "My thought was Napoleon. How is Johnny Carson like Napoleon?"

And the player has to come up with some "reasonable" answer, such as:

"They're both famous men who came from humble beginnings."

Or when you ask, "How is a pickle like Napoleon?" the player might say, "Both of them sometimes get cut."

Or to "How is a sick elephant like Napoleon?" one jokester might say that they both had a code in the head.

The answer can be ridiculous—the more ridiculous the better—but if it doesn't make any sense at all, or if the players can't come up with any answer, they have to pay a forfeit or drop out of the game.

When all the players have had a chance to explain their answers, it's someone else's turn to be "It," and new thoughts are needed all along the line.

The Minister's Cat

Players: 2 or more
Equipment: None
Preparation: None

This game is a very old one, and it seems so simple that you wonder at first why anyone would want to play it. Then, after a few rounds, you fall under its spell and realize why it has been popular for so many years.

Usually the game is played in a circle, with each person taking turns. If you're traveling, of course, you can set up any order you want—but that order has to be definite.

The Leader starts by saying, "The minister's cat is a _____ cat," filling in the blank with an adjective beginning with A. The leader could say, for example, "The minister's cat is an abominable cat."

Then the turn passes to the next person, who comes up with another adjective beginning with A for the cat: "The minister's cat is an aggravating cat," for instance.

And so it goes. Endless, you say? You think it will go on forever because there are so many adjectives beginning with A? Well, yes, you'd think so. But very rapidly, especially if you don't let anyone miss a beat, people start stumbling, missing, going blank, repeating what's been said, stuttering, getting tongues twisted up, and saying words beginning with the wrong letter. All of which means that they are OUT. If your group is small, though, and you want to play a longer game, you can allow them three misses before they have to drop out.

In any case, when someone misses, everyone shifts to the next letter. The next person in turn would start with something like, "The minister's cat is a beautiful cat"—or a boisterous cat—or a boring cat, etc.

THE MINISTER'S CAT IS ALL BAD

In this variation of the game, the adjectives all have to be negative. The minister's cat can't be agreeable, amiable, beautiful, bonny, charming, cute or anything else pleasant—only angry, awful, brash or bossy, cross or criminal or otherwise a rotten pet. This makes the game much tougher and more fun.

THE MINISTER'S CAT MOVES RIGHT ALONG

You'd think "The Minister's Cat" would be an easier game if you only had to come up with one single adjective with A and then the next person would come up with a B, and so on.

Well, it would be, if you didn't make other conditions for playing it. For example, you could decide ahead of time between you that the minister's cat was always going to be bad—or good—or from some country:

PLAYER #1: The minister's cat is an African cat.

PLAYER #2: The minister's cat is a Belgian cat.

PLAYER #3: The minister's cat is a Canadian cat.

Otherwise all the rules are the same. A flub and you're out, or you get a count against you. Five counts and you're out.

A is for Aardvark

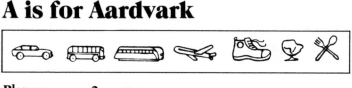

Players: 2 or more
Equipment: None
Preparation: None

This very silly alphabet game is another one of those quick contests that depends on your coming up with the right word at the right time. One player starts:

PLAYER #1: A is for Aardvark.
PLAYER #2: B bought it.
PLAYER #3: C cooked it.
PLAYER #4: D dunked it.
PLAYER #5: E elevated it.
PLAYER #6: F flossed it.
PLAYER #1: G gassed it.
PLAYER #2: H handled it.
PLAYER #3: I imitated it.
PLAYER #4: J jostled it.
PLAYER #5: K kissed it.
PLAYER #6: L loved it.
PLAYER #1: M missed it.
PLAYER #2: N needed it.
PLAYER #3: O opened it.
PLAYER #4: P punished it.
PLAYER #5: Q questioned it.
PLAYER #6: R ruffled it.
PLAYER #1: S stuffed it.
PLAYER #2: T tickled it.
PLAYER #3: U untied it.
PLAYER #4: V --- V ---

Player #4 is out. And so it goes. Don't try for X, Y and

Z. If you want to play the game again, just outlaw using the same words again. Or you can play it using longer answers, such as:

PLAYER #1: A is for Aardvark
PLAYER #2: B bought it candy
PLAYER #3: C called it a dummy
PLAYER #4: D did its hair
PLAYER #5: E ended its suffering

and so on.

The answers that the players come up with provide the entertainment in this one. Last person remaining in the game wins.

Categories

Players: 3 or more
Equipment: None
Preparation: None

Decide in what order the players will take their turns. Usually, the turns move around the circle, but it depends on how you're seated. Any order will do, but it has to be definite. Then the players set up a 6-beat rhythm. It goes like this:

- Tap your thighs twice.
- Clap your hands in front of you twice.
- Snap your fingers at about shoulder level twice.

All the players do this at the same time and no one stops or misses a beat.

Now, when you've got the rhythm going well, the first player begins by saying "Category" on one set of finger snaps, and then giving the name of a category on the next set of snaps. The category should be a broad one, such as trees or fruits or flowers, TV shows, desserts or breeds of dogs.

All the players keep up the tap-tap-clap-clap-snap-snap rhythm as the second player names something in the category on the next snap, ending the name by the time that second snap is over. Then the next player must give another name on the following snaps and so on, until somebody misses. It might go like this:

PLAYER #1 (*tap-tap, clap-clap*): Category (*As all snap; tap-tap, clap-clap*) Countries (*as they all snap*).

PLAYER #2 (*tap-tap, clap-clap*): England (*as they snap*).

PLAYER #3 (*tap-tap, clap-clap*): Australia (*as they snap*).

PLAYER #4 (*tap-tap, clap-clap*): Canada (*as they snap*).

PLAYER #1 (*tap-tap, clap-clap*): United States (*as they all snap*).

PLAYER #2 (*tap-tap, clap-clap*): Er -- (*as they all snap*).

PLAYER #2 is OUT.

Everyone gets the rhythm going again and Player #3 names a new category. Play on until only one person is left—the winner.

There's one more rule. You can't repeat a name that has already been given. That's no problem, you say? Well, wait until you're all set to say a particular thing and the player before you says it. You have about three seconds to come up with another name that hasn't been said before. Those snaps come fast, and it's hilarious to see the glazed eyes of a super-"Categories" player who has just dried up, blankly snapping fingers and not knowing what in the world is going to come out! Remember, if your tongue gets tangled up—or you garble your answer—that's an automatic out, too!

The Underhand Slap

Players: 2
Equipment: None
Preparation: None

This terrific little contest is wonderful for those times when you're waiting around, standing on line, and don't want to play another word game.

Face your opponent, placing your hands out in front of you at waist level, with fingers lightly outstretched. Keep your palms down.

Your opponent puts his or her hands right under yours, palms up. Your palms and those of your opponent should barely touch. Now you stare into each other's eyes.

The object of the game is for the underhand opponent to whip his or her hands out and hit the backs of yours before you can get your hands away. In order to accomplish this, your opponent has to be very sly and very fast, because the moment you get the idea that you're about to get slapped, you're going to get your hands out of there! How do you know you're going to get slapped? Not only from the movement of the palms under yours, but also from the gleam in the eye of your opponent—a glint that is always there before a hit—unless you're dealing with a world-class underhand slapper!

Once you get hit, change positions and you become the underhand slapper.

Score 2 points for striking both hands, 1 for striking one hand. But the fun isn't in the score or the win. It's in that moment-to-moment eye-to-eye combat!

House That Jack Built

Players: 2 or more
Equipment: None
Preparation: None

This giggly sort of game is very like the nursery rhyme, "The House that Jack Built." The first player makes a statement and the second player adds on a phrase. The players continue taking turns, and each one must repeat accurately all that has been said as well as adding a new phrase. None of the statements needs to be true, and the funnier the better.

For example:

I have a car.

I have a chauffeur who loves the car.

I have a maid who loves the chauffeur who loves the car.

I have a dish that was cracked by the maid who loves the chauffeur who loves the car.

I have a boy who smashed the dish that was cracked by the maid . . .

And so on. Any player who misses is out.

5
Pencil & Paper Games

From the familiar games you learned to play as a tot—to the trickiest tactics, graphics and word-building—these pencil gymnastics will keep you busy for as long as you want. They're great for playing on the plane, easy to stop and start up again, and all you need—besides a paper and pencil—is a playmate in the next seat.

Dots

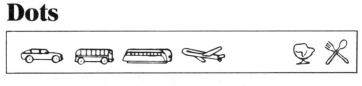

Players: 2
Equipment: Pencil and paper
Preparation: None

Take a sheet of paper and make as many rows of dots as you want—10 or more dots in each direction. Then each player takes a turn and draws a line connecting one dot with the next in any direction—except diagonally—and in any part of the diagram.

Try to connect the dots so that they make little squares. When you draw a line that finishes a square, you initial the closed square and then draw an extra line. The player with the most initialed squares wins.

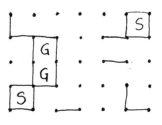

Eternal Triangles

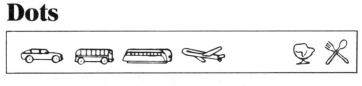

Players: 2
Equipment: Pencil and paper
Preparation: None

This game is similar to "Dots." Cover a sheet of paper

with dots starting with one in the first row, 2 in the second, 3 in the third, and so on as far as you care to go, as in the diagram here.

Each player in turn draws a line connecting two of the dots either horizontally or diagonally, and the object is to form an enclosed triangle. When you add the line that forms the enclosed triangle, initial it and go again. The game is over when one of you fails to form a triangle.

The player who makes the most triangles wins.

You can make this game more difficult if you score extra points for larger triangles (made up of small triangles with your initials only). Score them up at the end of the game.

Snakes

Players:	**2–4**
Equipment:	**Pencil and paper**
Preparation:	**None**

Here is another relative of "Dots."

Set up a bunch of dots on your paper, the same

way you did for the previous games. Now, starting anywhere you like, take turns drawing in lines from dot to dot, but don't make boxes. Instead, make a long, stiff snake. No diagonal lines allowed. No skipping spaces.

The winner is the last one to be able to draw a line without connecting the snake to itself.

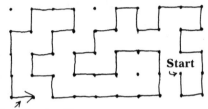

The winning line

Doodlebug

Players: 2
Equipment: Paper and pencil for each player
Preparation: None

Each player draws the following diagram:

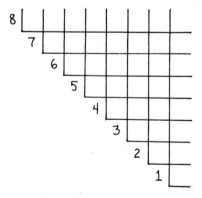

Choose to see who goes first. The first player—
Eve—writes a number between 1 and 8, not in one of
the boxes, but elsewhere on her paper. She shields her
pencil and paper with her other hand, trying to hide
what she has written from the other player—Adam. If
Adam can guess the number Eve wrote, he gets to
write it in the appropriate line of his diagram, and it
is his turn to write a hidden number. If Adam guesses
wrong, Eve gets to place the number on the appropriate line of her diagram, and she gets another turn.

Note: Cross off the hidden doodle numbers
after each turn so that no arguments can
arise about which number was just written.

The object of the game is to be the player who fills
all the boxes of the diagram first. The diagram will
then contain eight 8's, seven 7's, six 6's, etc.

Hint: When you doodle a number, either
hold your pencil as still as possible so as not
to give a clue to the number, or move it
wildly to confuse your opponent.

Battleships

Players: 2
Equipment: **Paper and pencil for each player.
              (Use graph paper if available. It
              saves time and effort and it's
              neater.)**
Preparation: **Each player makes up a 10-square
              chart (see next page).**

The object of this popular game is to sink the enemy's
ships before the enemy can sink yours.

Each player has
a battleship—made up of 5 squares
a cruiser—made up of 4 squares
a destroyer—made up of 3 squares
a nuclear sub—made up of 2 squares

The first thing each player does is to hide his or her ship chart. Draw the ships' outlines into your hidden chart, like this:

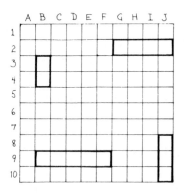

Ships can be placed horizontally or vertically, not diagonally.

War is declared.

The first player—Jean—calls out a square by letter and number, say F5.

The other player—Mike—must tell her whether or not it is a hit. Look at the sample game shown here; you see that it was a miss. Jean puts an O in that box, to show that it was called and it was a miss.

Now it's Mike's turn. He calls B3, which just happens to be Jean's nuclear sub. Jean admits it is a hit, but she doesn't tell Mike what *kind* of ship he hit. Mike puts a big X in that square in his chart, Jean shades hers.

It's Jean's turn. She calls another square, D6—a hit, Mike tells her. It is his destroyer, but he doesn't tell her that. Jean puts an X in D6. Mike shades D6 in his chart.

Mike's turn. He calls B4. Why? Mike knows that at least one other square is connected to the first hit, since no ship fits in less than 2 squares. It is a hit. But this time, Jean must not only admit to the hit, she must admit that the ship is sunk. Now Mike knows that he sank Jean's submarine, so he darkens in both submarine squares. He knows from that that he doesn't have to try to make more hits right around that area. The next time Mike's turn comes up, he'll be wise to call a square on the other side of the chart, or further down.

The charts now look like this:

Jean's chart   **Mike's chart**

The game goes on in the same way until one player has sunk all the other player's ships.

About the charts: This game is often played with each player keeping up two charts, one to represent his or her own ships and the squares the enemy has called, and the other to show the calls the player has made and the hits scored. The two-chart method may be helpful when an adult is playing with a small child who may make mistakes in recording his or her own hits. Then the adult can help clear up any confusion. Otherwise, one chart seems to do the job very well.

Hangman

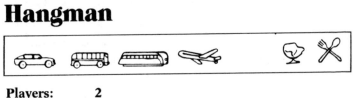

Players: 2
Equipment: Paper and paper
Preparation: None

You need to know how to play "Hangman," in order to play "Hangman Grows Up." Just in case you don't know, here is a speedy explanation. (Also see the diagrams on page 87.)

Draw a gallows (an upside down L), think of a word (don't say it aloud) and dash off a string of dashes, one for each letter in the word. Then print the alphabet at the bottom of the page.

Your opponent must guess, one letter at a time, the word you've chosen. If a guess of a letter is correct, write it at the appropriate place and strike it off in the alphabet below. If the letter appears in your word more than once, put it in wherever it belongs.

If your opponent guesses wrong, strike the letter out of the alphabet and draw in a head at the end of the gallows.

For each wrong letter guessed, draw in another body part; two more wrong guesses would give two eyes; another two would supply ears, a sixth would give a mouth; the seventh a torso, and the next four would add arms and legs. If you want to make the game longer, go on to hands and shoes.

Note: Long, complicated words are easier, not harder than short words. Short words containing the less frequently used letters are the most difficult to guess, words such as *why, fox, bay, ski, tax,* and even *yore.* Even if your opponent guessed *o-r-e* quickly, think of all the letters that would probably come up before getting to Y!

HANGMAN GROWS UP

Once you have become expert at "Hangman," you'll be ready for "Hangman Grows Up." Instead of just words, use other categories in the dashes. You might do it with proverbs, famous sayings, books, movies or plays. How about famous people in history? Athletes? Song titles? The possibilities are endless. But because you get more clues than in regular "Hangman," two parts are hung every time you miss.

DOUBLE HANGING

If an adult and child are playing together, they might want to try this variation on the game to make it more of a contest.

When it is the younger player's turn, he or she chooses two words and strings them out under the gallows. Then as the adult guesses, the younger one puts in the letters wherever they belong in both words. But when a letter appears in only one of the words a part is hung for the miss on the other word. If the letter appears in neither word, two parts are hung.

G H O S T   M O U S E

A B C D E F G H I J K L M N O P Q R S T U V W X Y Z

Tic-Tac-Toe Squared

Players: 2
Equipment: Paper and pencil
Preparation: None

You probably know how to play "Tic-tac-toe" ("Noughts and Crosses"). It's played in a large square divided into nine small squares.

Each of two players in turn places his or her mark—an X or an O—in a small square.

The first player to get three marks in a horizontal, vertical, or diagonal line wins.

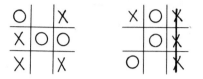

But "Tic-tac-toe Squared" will be a bit more of a challenge. Make the same tic-tac-toe box that you always make, but then close the edges:

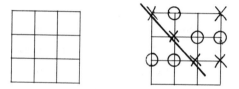

And play the X's and O's on the intersections instead of in the boxes. You need 3 in a row to win.

TIC-TAC-TOE-TOE

If you get tired of "Tic-Tac-Toe Squared," try this variation. Draw five lines across and five lines down, for a 4-box playing area (16 boxes in all):

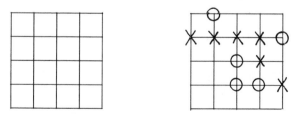

And play the X's and the O's on the intersection again, but this time you need four in a row to win.

Go-Bang

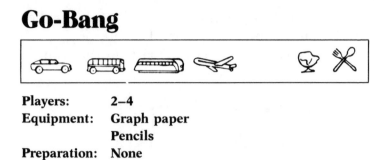

Players:	2–4
Equipment:	Graph paper
	Pencils
Preparation:	None

There are lots of names for this game. People play it all over the world and call it something different. Even within the same country it is often called by several names.

You can play it on paper or on a pegboard with pegs or on a checkerboard—on any surface that is marked off in boxes. If you play it on paper, it is much easier to use graph paper.

The object of the game is to take turns writing in X's and O's, as in "Tic-Tac-Toe Squared," until you get five X's or five O's in a row. If you are a skillful player, this game can go on and on!

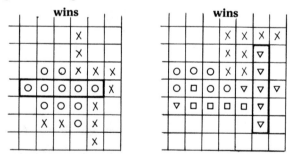

Hint: Beware of a row of X's or O's. When you see it, quickly stop it with your mark, because once your opponent gets four in a row—with nothing limiting it on either end—the game is over.

Three people or four can play this game, but it is best as a contest for two players. If you play with as many as four, use triangles and squares as well as X's and O's.

Cat-astrophe

Players: **2 or more**
Equipment: **Paper and pencil for each player**
Preparation: **None**

For a long-playing pencil and paper game, choose a simple 3-letter word like "cat." Set a time limit of from 15 to 30 minutes, and at a signal, start listing as many words as possible containing the word you've decided on. The word may occur in any part of the longer word, but it must be intact.

For instance, if "cat," is your word, you may use *catastrophe, cater, abdicate, prevaricate, scatter*, etc., but not *castle* or *intact*.

If you choose the word "pen," your list might contain *penny, repent, open*, etc.

The player with the longest list is the winner.

Gibberish

Players: 2 or more
Equipment: Paper and pencil for each player
Preparation: None

Each player writes out a well-known proverb, running the letters all together, like this:

Astitchintimesavesnine.

Now break it up at odd intervals, like this:

Ast it chint imesa vesni ne.

Exchange papers and see who can be first to write out the proverb correctly. If you want to make the game last longer, each can write a number of proverbs, 5 apiece, or even 10—for the others to solve. You might find yourself looking at what seems to be a brand new conglomeration but turns out to be the same proverb you have given your opponent!

Every Other

Players: 2 or more
Equipment: Paper and pencil for each player
Preparation: None

Crossword puzzle fans like playing this game.

Armed with pencil and paper, each player makes out a list of 10 words (or any number you agree on), but omits every other letter. To put it another way, write down every other letter, starting with the second letter of each word you've chosen. Then, next to each word, write a synonym or brief definition—preferably humorous or tricky. Then switch papers. Winner is the one with the most correct answers.

A sample list might contain:

- I - F - R - N - E   meaning REMAINDER (difference)

- I - T - O -A - Y   meaning WORDY BOOK (dictionary)

- A - H - O - A - L   meaning OF THE LATEST STYLE (fashionable)

As you can see, it's easier to make them up than to puzzle them out! Set a time limit for each phase of the game, and after you've played it a few times, try playing without any definitions!

Longest Word

Players: 2 or more
Equipment: Paper and pencil for each player
Preparation: None

You start this game with a one-letter word (A or I) and

add letters one at a time. Each time you add a new letter it must form another word, and at no time can you change the order of the previous letters. But you may add the new letter at the beginning or the end, or insert it anywhere inside the word. The object is to see who can form the longest word.

Here is a sample game:

A
AY
SAY
STAY
STRAY
ASTRAY
ASHTRAY
ASHTRAYS

When you arrive at the final word, tell it to your opponents but don't let them see your worksheet. They must then play the game in reverse and take the letters away one by one until they arrive back at the original one-letter word.

Word Steps

Players: 1 or more
Equipment: Paper and pencil for each player
Preparation: None

How many steps from lamb to wolf? We made it in eight.

The idea is to progress from one word to another by changing one letter at a time. With each one-letter change, you must form a new word. For instance, this is one way to get from lamb to wolf:

lamb
lame
same
sale
sole
sold
gold
golf
wolf

Maybe you can do it in fewer steps.

Start by selecting a pair of 4-letter words at random—or you can choose a pair with amusing or contrasting association. Both players write down the same pair of words, and set a time limit of 5 or 10 minutes. Now see who can get from one to the other in the fewest steps. In case of a tie, the one who finishes first is the winner.

Sprouts

Players: 2
Equipment: Paper and pencil
Preparation: None

This game is a bit like "Dots" (page 80), because you

connect the dots, and because the object of the game is to leave your opponent unable to make a move.

But instead of a page full of dots, you start with just three or four anywhere on the page. And in addition to straight lines, you can draw

arcs

curves

loops

or squiggles

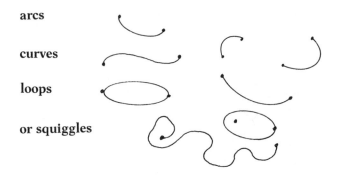

as you join the dots.

You can join two dots together—or make a loop joining one dot to itself.

Every time you draw a line, arc, curve, loop or squiggle, you have to add a new dot (shown here as a larger white circle so you can see it more easily) somewhere on the line (NOT necessarily in the middle).

What's the catch? You may not cross a line

dotted line is illegal

and no blop may have more than 3 sprouts coming out of it. As soon as you attach your third sprout to the blop, put a slash through it (it makes it easier to see) so that you know that blop is out of play. When you get expert, you may decide to leave the slashes out.

The winner is the one who makes the last possible move.

Here is a game you might play:

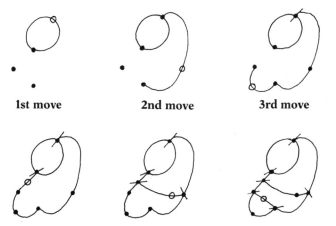

1st move	2nd move	3rd move

4th move	5th move	6th move

7th move

Even though 2 blops are still alive, you cannot play them without crossing a line or connecting to a dead blop. The game is over.

Part of the fun of Sprouts is that while you're sprouting and blopping, you're creating a very weird picture. Try it!

Word Bridges

Players: 2 or more
Equipment: Paper and pencil for each player
Preparation: None

Be an architect of words and see who can build the longest word bridge with pencil and paper. Each player draws 6 horizontal lines across the paper, and then one gets first choice in selecting a word of 6 letters. Write the word vertically down the page, one letter at the beginning of each line. Then write the word up from the bottom, one letter at the *end* of each line.

```
F   . . . . . . . . . . . . . . . . .   R
E   . . . . . . . . . . . . . . . . .   E
N   . . . . . . . . . . . . . . . .     D
D   ISINTEGRATIO                        N
E   _____                   E
R   _____                   F
```

Each game lasts 3 minutes. At the word "Go" you each start to fill in the 6 bridges with words starting and ending with the letters that are already there. The longer the word the better. When the game is over, you score as follows:

The player with the longest word for each bridge gets 5 points. Then add up the total number of letters used for all 6 words. The player with the highest total score subtracts the next highest score and adds the difference to his or her total score. The first player to win 50 points, or 100 points, if you want to play a longer game, is the winner.

6
At the Table

How many times—especially when you're travelling and have to eat out a lot—have you been stuck at the table with nothing to do? It happens while you wait to be waited on, while you wait for your food, while you wait for dessert, while you wait for the bill. You can play most of these games while you're waiting in restaurants, if the people you're sitting with don't object.

Actually, you can play most of them anywhere else, too, while you're waiting, so long as you have a table or desk space. They're best of all for airport cafeterias—interesting enough to keep you awake and intrigued while you're waiting for an announcement or a gate number to go up, but not long enough or involved enough to make you miss your plane.

Making a Paper Cup You Can Drink From

Players:	1
Equipment:	A sheet of paper (square)
Preparation:	The ideal sheet of paper for making the paper cup is 8½ × 8½ (216mm × 216mm). Where do you get a sheet that weird size? If you have two sheets of 8½ × 11 notebook paper (216mm × 280mm)—but no ruler—use one of the sheets to measure off 8½ inches against the other, like this:

8½" (216 mm)

11"
(280 mm)

8½"
(216 mm)

No, this isn't a game, but it's such a valuable thing to know how to do that it belongs in any book about travelling.

Have you ever been stuck without a cup or glass? It happens quite a lot. Sometimes the hotel or motel doesn't leave enough glasses. Sometimes you filled them with something else. Of maybe you're outside and want to scoop up some water from a fountain or a stream. This is how to make a paper cup that will hold water, and all you need is one sheet of paper.

1. Fold the sheet diagonally.

2. Take the top end (a) and fold it (dotted line) so that it meets the center of the opposite side (d).

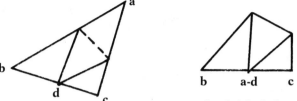

3. Make a sharp crease. Turn over the folded sheet. It looks a little like a kite.

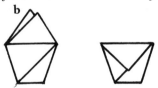

4. Fold the bottom end (c) so that it meets the top of the kite, like this:

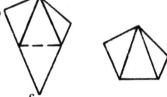

5. Now you have two points at the top (b). Fold one down toward you and the other away from you.

That's all! To use the cup, give it a little squeeze along the sharp sides. You'll find it opens up and is ready for action.

Warning: Not too much action. The cup may not last long—depending on the kind of paper you use to make it. Don't fill it too full, and be watchful for leaks.

Table Football

Players:	2 (more can play in round robin tournaments)
Equipment:	A sheet of paper
	Table (ideal length for beginners is at least 40 inches or 1 meter, but you can play on a table of any length)
	Any flat surface, such as a book or ruler
Preparation:	Using the sheet of paper, make the football as follows:

Illus. 1

Fold the sheet of paper in half lengthwise.

Then fold it again lengthwise.

Fold over one edge.

And fold again and again as you would a flag.

Football

Tuck the edge into the football.

Flip a coin to see who goes first.

The first move: Set the football on end at the edge of the table as in Illus. 2:

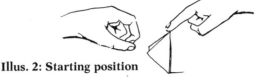

Illus. 2: Starting position

Or lay it flat—part on and part off the table—as shown in Illus. 3.

Illus. 3: Alternative starting position

The first to play then flicks it with a finger or shoves it across the table. The object is to get the football *just exactly* on the edge of the opponent's side of the table, with one edge of the football sticking over the end of the table—*without going off*. This is a "touchdown" and it is worth six points.

Illus. 4: Touchdown

Your opponent, without changing the position of the football, flicks it back with the same idea in mind.

The play continues, with players taking turns.

The Rules

1. If you hit the ball off the table, you are charged with a "down."

It is up to your opponent then, to put the ball back in play, starting as in Illus. 2 or 3, from his or her end of the table.

2. When you have been charged with four "downs" of your own, you are "out" and your opponent gets a chance for a field goal. (See Rule 6.)

3. Touchdown: When you get a touchdown, it is worth 6 points and a try at an extra point. This "try" is a chance to make a field goal. (See Rule 6.)

4. You may not hit the football with your thumb or cover the football with your hand at any point during the game.

5. You may not pick up the football in the middle of play, unless you shoot it off the table, and are charged with a "down."

6. Field goal procedure: When you have been charged with three downs—before you are forced out—you can try for a field goal. You also get to try for one after you score a touchdown. For this you need to set up goal posts, which are created by putting your fingers in the position shown below:

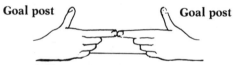

Illus. 5: Goal post position

Then the one who is doing the finger-kicking sets up the ball on end (as in the starting position, illus. 2), approximately 3 inches (7.5 cm) from the edge of the table, and tries to send it above the bar and between the goal posts that the opponent is holding steady.

To avoid arguments, the kicker is the one to decide whether the kick is good or not.

A field goal is worth 3 points, unless it takes place after a touchdown, in which case it is worth only one extra point, just as in field football.

After a field goal, your opponent starts the ball back in play, beginning at his or her edge of the table (with the ball in position as in Illus. 2 or 3).

Penny Soccer

Players: 2

Equipment: 3 or more coins. (You can play with all pennies or any other group of coins. Playing with a variety of coins in the same game is more interesting.)
A table
2 pens or pencils

Preparation: None

You, sitting at one end of the table are the Defender. You place your index finger and pinky on the edge of the table, with your middle fingers bent underneath (like this):

Goal

Backboard

Illus. 1

The space between your fingers on the table is the Goal.

Your opponent—the Attacker—sits at the other end of the table, and arranges the pennies in either this order:

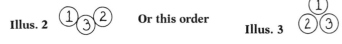

Illus. 2   **Or this order**   **Illus. 3**

The first move: The Attacker—with four fingers bent—pushes, or flip-pushes the pennies, just enough to break the formation and prepare for the next move.

Illus. 4

The second move and all the moves after that, are used to maneuver a penny into the Defender's goal. The Attacker may use any finger or fingers to shoot the penny through, but *not* his or her thumb. The Attacker gets as many turns as it takes (no one counts), as long as the Attacker doesn't break any rules.

The Rules

1. The penny that the Attacker shoots must go in a path between the other two pennies.

2. The penny must not touch either one.

3. The penny may not go off the table.

4. To be a goal, the penny must hit your knuckles on the table edge.

5. If the Attacker has a difficult shot to make—a curve, for example—the player may use a pen or pencil to assist the shot. In Illus. 5 you see the problem the Attacker is up against.

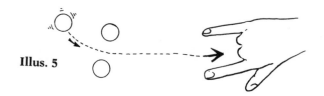

Illus. 5

In Illus. 6 you see how a pen can be used to solve it.

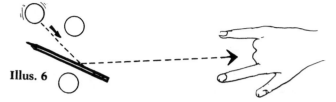

Illus. 6

The players take turns trying to shoot a goal. If the Attacker breaks one of the rules, his or her turn is over and the Defender becomes the Attacker. The next time the opponent's turn comes up, the game begins all over again with the basic penny formation.

The player who makes the most goals, after an equal number of turns, wins.

Playing with More Than 3 coins

If you use more than 3 coins (you can use any number), begin with a pyramid formation like this:

Illus. 7

When you attack you must always designate the two coins you are shooting between. If your coin hits another coin on the table, your turn ends.

PENNY SOCCER FOR EXPERTS

Choose one of three pennies as the one you will shoot into the goal. Turn it heads up while the other two are tails up, or vice versa. If you score any other penny, your turn continues, but it does not count as a goal.

At the Table • 107

Flip the Box

Players: 2 or more
Equipment: A matchbox
Preparation: If the matchbox has the same design on top and bottom, you'll need to mark it in some way so that you can tell which face is which. You can do that with a marker, with a piece of tape, or by slipping a narrow strip of napkin inside it, letting the edge of it protrude slightly outside the box.

Set the matchbox at the edge of the table, so that about a third of it sticks out over the table edge. Then using your index finger, flick it upwards. You can do this with your palm down or up, but always start the flick from your thumb:

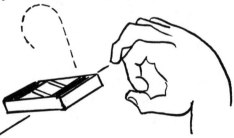

and flick the bottom of the box. Score 0 if the box lands top side down, 1 if it lands top up, 5 if it lands on its side, 10 if it lands on end.

You can play until it's time to leave, and then the one with the higher score wins. Or you can decide on the winning score before you start.

Cootie

	🍵 🍴

Players: 2 or more
Equipment: A sugar cube—or any other object with 6 equal sides.
Paper and pencil
Preparation: On each side of the cube, write a letter:
B (stands for Body)
H (stands for Head)
L (stands for Leg)
E (stands for Eye)
A (stands for Antenna)
T (stands for Tail)

It's very sad that this game isn't played much anymore, but you don't find many restaurants these days that serve sugar cubes! And it isn't easy to find other objects with six sides. You can, of course, play it with dice, letting a number stand for each part. But how often do we carry around dice when we're travelling?

In any case, "Cootie" is a fun game and shouldn't be lost completely. Here's how you play: It's similar to "Hangman" (page 86) in one way: you draw a creature step-by-step, and when the drawing is completed, the game is over. But in "Hangman" you draw a person, and in "Cootie," you draw a flea.

In order to start your picture going, you roll the cube out of a cup onto the table. As soon as you roll a B (body) you can begin your drawing. This entitles you to another turn. But the next letter you come up with must be something that you can add to your picture. For example, if you throw an A for antenna or an E for eye, you can't add it, and you lose your turn. But, if you threw a head, leg or tail, you could add any one of them easily, and you'd get another turn.

In order to complete your cootie, you'll need to throw
1 Body
1 Head
6 Legs
2 Eyes
2 Antennae
1 Tail

First finished cootie wins and scores 13 points, 1 for each cootie part. Other players can total up the cootie parts they've drawn in order to come up with their score.

A finished cootie looks like this:

The Simplest Solitaire Game

Players: 1 or more
Equipment: A deck of playing cards
Preparation: None

This is one of the only card games it's possible to play in a plane without getting messed up, dropping cards, and generally being sorry you started. It's super simple and you don't even have to have a table in order to play.

Turn over the cards, one at a time. As you turn them over count aloud: Ace, Two, Three, Four and so on—a word for every card. The object of the game is to get through the entire deck without ever saying the correct name of the card that you're turning over. If you should happen to be saying "Three," for example, while you're turning over a three, you have to stop, and your score is only the number of cards you've already turned up. You can play 5 rounds of this game and tally up your score—or play against an opponent with whom you take turns.

The Sugar Game

Players:	**2 or more**
Equipment:	**3 packets of sugar for every player (or artificial sweetener packets, or pebbles, or pieces of a drinking straw, or matches)**
Preparation:	**None**

This wonderful game is perfect for those times when you're waiting to be served at a restaurant. I've always suspected that the waiters didn't look too kindly on our family crushing and mutilating 12 of their sugar packets, but no one ever complained about it to us. As a matter of fact, I think many of them were interested in the game.

Each player puts none, one, two or three of their packets into one fist, which is held out toward the other players. The other packets stay hidden in the other fist. When everyone is holding out a fist, the guessing starts. Each player guesses how many objects there are in total in all the fists being held out. Each one must guess a different number. Then, when the fists open up, the person who guessed right is the winner. One win scores one point. Highest number of points when the food comes, wins.

The Penny Game

Players: **2 or more**
Equipment: **5–10 pennies per player (or matches, pebbles, pieces of a drinking straw or napkin scraps)**
Preparation: **None**

This game is similar to "The Sugar Game." Your opponent holds out a fist with some of the 10 pennies in it. Then you have to guess whether the number of pennies is odd or even. If you're right, you win a penny. If you're not, you pay a penny. Then it's your turn to hold out a fist. The one with the most pennies when the food comes wins.

7

The World's Most Challenging Games

Why call these the world's most challenging games? Because they test your imagination as well as your skill at guessing and remembering and sensing things.

And once your imagination is at work, there's no limit to how interesting, complicated, surprising and electrifying the play can be.

If you like to write, sketch, invent—or experiment with ideas—investigate this section.

Essences

Players: 2 or more
Equipment: None
Preparation: None

The most fascinating of all guessing games, Essences calls on your intuition, imagination and logic—all at the same time.

Before the game begins, the players agree on what kind of subject will be used—whether it will be a famous person or fictional character, or someone that everyone in the group knows (it could be someone who is present), which is the most fun. Then one player thinks of a person and it's up to the others to identify him or her by finding out the "essence" of the person. There is no limit on number of questions.

Here is a sample game:

BOB: I am thinking of a fictional character who is male. (*His subject is Ebenezer Scrooge from Dickens' A Christmas Carol.*)

DOROTHY: What music is this person?

BOB: Discordant modern music.

DALE: What kind of animal is this person?

BOB: A skinny anteater.

MARJORIE: What color is this person?

BOB: Grey.

DOROTHY: What article of wearing apparel?

BOB: An old sweater. (BOB *resisted the impulse to say an old dressing gown, which is what is associated with Scrooge, but not what his essence is.*)

DALE: What kind of tree?

BOB: An old gnarled oak with most of its branches gone.

As you can see, no one can say whether your answers are right or wrong; they are just your impression of what the character is like. At some point in the questions, the guessers will want to summarize what they feel about the character you've described, and you can set them more on the right track if you think you've led them astray with some of your impressions. Generally, it's amazing how accurately they describe your character! They can take any number of guesses to identify it, too. And you're as happy as they are when they get it right.

Other categories you can ask about:

what recreational event	what dessert
what restaurant	what country
what kind of dog	what book
what piece of furniture	what kind of film
what fruit	(western, horror, etc.)
what flower	what sport
what mineral	what facial feature
what kind of house	what car
what part of the body	what time of day

Time flies by and so do the miles with this intriguing game. Even the driver can play.

Psychic Experiments

Players: 2
Equipment: A magazine with full page illustrations
Preparation: None

Are you psychic? What better time to find out than when you're shut off from most distractions? This is a splendid game for bus, train or plane where all the usual preoccupations have been removed.

Select a magazine and open it to an illustration, but keep the picture hidden from your partner. Then ask a specific question about it, such as, "How many people (or animals or houses or windows) are in the picture I'm looking at?"

Now concentrate as hard as you can on the people in the illustration while your partner tries to clear his or her mind and allow the picture to come through. The answer you get may be right or wrong, but in either case, go on to another question. Don't make a guessing game of it. If the answer is wrong, just say, "No, there are two people. Now I'm going to concentrate on what one of them is doing. Try to tell me what that is." And then go on to other questions.

The results may truly astound you, especially if the first answer happens to be correct. Researchers have found that people who think they have psychic abilities are able to do far better in ESP experiments than people who think they haven't—or that ESP doesn't exist. So the confidence you build up by getting an answer right can actually give great impetus to your psychic powers.

If you don't seem to be getting anywhere, change roles and let your partner choose the magazine and the illustration—and "send" the picture out to you. Sometimes it works better one way than the other.

Mind Over Money

Players:	2
Equipment:	A coin
	Score sheet
Preparation:	None

Can the mind influence inanimate objects and make them conform to its will? This is your chance to find out.

Take a coin. If you flip it a great many times, you should come out with an average of 50 heads and 50 tails in every 100 flips, according to the Law of Averages. The more trials you make, the closer to an exact 50–50 you will come.

But suppose you have the power to influence the flip of the coin and cause it to turn up heads—or tails—a disproportionate number of times. Then you'd be upsetting the Law of Averages!

To try your powers, let one person concentrate on either heads or tails. The other keeps track of the number of tosses, and the number of times the coin turns up "right." Decide for yourself when you are the "influencer," whether you prefer to have the other person flip the coin, or whether you wish to flip it yourself and, perhaps, influence it more directly.

Writing Charades

Players: 2 or more
Equipment: Pencil and paper
Preparation: None

You probably know how to play "Charades": You are assigned the title of a book, a song, a movie, a play— or you are given a proverb or saying—and you act it out, word by word (sometimes syllable by syllable), so that your team can guess it in the shortest possible time.

"Writing Charades" is a little different. Instead of acting out the name of whatever it is, you draw it. For example, *A Tale of Two Cities* might look like this:

"Little pitchers have big ears" might look like this:

And "On Top of Old Smoky" might be:

Not all subjects are as easy to draw as those, however. You might get something like "I've been Working on the Railroad," and choose to illustrate it word by word:

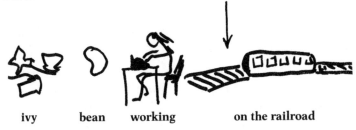

ivy   bean   working   on the railroad

If just two people are playing, there isn't anyone to assign a subject, so you each simply decide what you're going to draw. Then trade papers and decipher each other's creations.

If you're playing with more than three other people, you can form two teams. Each team thinks up a really tough subject, writes it down and passes it along to a member of the opposing team. That person must draw the subject so clearly that the remaining team members can guess it fast. Both teams can play simultaneously, or go one at a time while the other team watches.

If you play this way, one team can time the other, limiting the number of minutes anyone can take to think up a subject, to draw it and guess it. Speediest wins!

Word Associations

Players: 2 or more
Equipment: None
Preparation: None

The first player names a noun. The second player has to answer with a word associated with it. For example, let's say the first player says, "Cat." The second player (you) might say, "Dog." Here the association is obvious—both are pets—and the answer gets you one point.

But what if you didn't say, "Dog"? What if you said, "Hat"? The first player might challenge you. And when you're challenged, you have to come up with a good reason why your answer is a valid choice. You might explain that you were thinking of Dr. Seuss's *The Cat in the Hat*, which would be a fine answer. A successful challenger gets two points, while an unsuccessful challenger loses two points. So, if the first player did challenge you, he or she would end up with −2 (minus two) points for that round. And as a successful defender, you'd end up with +2. (Of course, if you had lost the challenge, you would have lost those points, as well.)

As you can see, an obvious answer is safe and will always get you one point. But a subtle answer—one that gets challenged—can put you 4 points ahead. It pays to be crafty!

If you're playing with more than two people, the third player would then go next with an association to the word "Hat." If only two were playing, the first player would go next with an association to "Hat."

Majority vote decides whether an answer is valid. If only two are playing, you can either work it out between you or let a third party decide.

My Grandmother's Trunk

Players: 2 or more
Equipment: None
Preparation: None

Poor Grandma travelled with the strangest collection of stuff. Once she took a trip, and in her trunk she carried fruit, feathers, foreign cars, fake jewelry, a fountain and some other surprising objects. On another trip her trunk contained pillows, parsley, portraits, penguins, a psychiatrist and, oddly enough, pajamas.

To play the game, the first player starts by mentioning one item that Grandma carried in her trunk. The next player repeats this item and adds another item that must start with the same letter.

Each time a new item is added, the player must repeat the whole list, starting with the first item, before adding on a new one, again an item starting with the same letter. The list must be said in the exact order. First person to make a mistake loses.

For a slightly more difficult game, don't start all Grandma's stuff with the same letter. Let her take anything at all with her!

My Lady's Lapdog

Players:	2 or more
Equipment:	None
Preparation:	None

This memory game may remind you of the song, "The Twelve Days of Christmas," but instead of "A partridge in a pear tree," it keeps coming back to "My lady's lapdog."

The first player says, "My lady's lapdog."

The second player says, "Two ____ ____ and my lady's lapdog"—filling in two of any things that begin with the same letter, say, "two fat fillies."

The next player adds three of something—perhaps "three silly sandwiches," and goes on to repeat, "Two fat fillies and my lady's lapdog."

And so on. The fourth player might say:

"Four happy hikers, three silly sandwiches, two fat fillies and my lady's lapdog."

Keep the game going for as long as you like—or as long as you can—whichever comes first!

MY LADY'S LAPDOG: Expert's Game

Want a challenge? Instead of making the letters agree (Fat fillies, Happy hikers), choose completely unrelated words. A game might go like this:

#1 PLAYER: My lady's lapdog.

#2 PLAYER: Two thoroughbred frogs and my lady's lapdog.

#3 PLAYER: Three purple sandwiches, two thoroughbred frogs and my lady's lapdog.

#4 PLAYER: Four Egyptian hikers, three purple sandwiches, two thoroughbred frogs and my lady's lapdog.

And so on. It's much tougher!

The Ultimate Memory Game

Players: 2 or more
Equipment: None
Preparation: None

You might remember Jane Fonda and Vanessa Redgrave playing a variation of this game in the movie, *Julia*. It seems like the other memory games in this chapter at first glance. But instead of simply stringing ideas together, this intriguing game gets you telling a story. If you're interested in words or images or storytelling, and if the minds of the players are in sync, it can be a really creative and stimulating game.

The first player starts with a simple sentence—a sentence with no adjectives or phrases in it—something like, "I am an actor," or "I went to Alaska." The sentence should have a noun in it that starts with A.

The second player repeats that sentence, but adds a phrase that contains the letter B. For example:

PLAYER #1: I am an actor. . . .

PLAYER #2: I am an actor in Budapest. . . .

PLAYER #3: I am an actor in Budapest, playing comedies. . . .

And so on, through the alphabet.

Any player who cannot remember the story or continue it, drops out.

Once two players have dropped out, they start their own game. The others, as they too drop out, join them. So the game continues, until all are out except the winner. Then the winner joins the second game.

THE ULTIMATE MEMORY GAME— in Midstream

In this variation on the game, you can start anywhere in the alphabet. For example:

PLAYER #1: I have a dream. . . .

PLAYER #2: I have a dream of eternity. . . .

PLAYER #3: I have a dream of eternity and free-dom. . . .

PLAYER #4: I have a dream of eternity and free-dom among the ghosts of the past. . . .

And so on. The only advantage to starting later in the alphabet is that you get a chance to use different letters than the usual A, B and C—and different words.

THE ULTIMATE MEMORY GAME— FREE FORM

In this variation on the game there are no restrictions! No restrictions on nouns or on letters or on anything else. You can take turns building the story in any way you want. For instance:

PLAYER #1: I used to love to go sailing. . . .

PLAYER #2: (*can continue with another phrase or a whole new sentence*): I used to love to go sailing on a Chinese junk . . .

PLAYER #3: I used to love to go sailing on a Chinese junk. Until that day when I met the magician. . . .

PLAYER #4: I used to love to go sailing on a Chinese junk. Until that day when I met the magician who practised the black arts. . . .

Getting interesting? Try finishing it yourself!

Age Range Chart & Index

Game	Page	Ages 6–8	8–12	13–18	Adult
A Is for Aardvark	73		★	★	★
Alphabet on Road & Track	31		★	★	★
Backward Alphabet	64		★	★	★
Battleships	83	★	★		
Botticelli	20		★	★	★
Botticelli for Experts	22			★	★
Bus Stop Game	24	★	★		
Car Lotto	34	★	★		
Car of Your Choice	31		★	★	
Cat-Astrophe	91		★	★	★
Categories	74		★	★	★
Cheeseburger	67		★	★	★
Coffeepot	18		★	★	★
Collecting Cars	24	★	★	★	★
Cootie	109	★	★		
Dance Daringly in Denmark	52		★	★	★
Doodlebug	82		★		
Double Hanging	88	★	★		
Dots	80	★	★		
Eagle Eye	32	★	★	★	★
End Games	57		★	★	★
Essences	114		★	★	★
Eternal Triangles	80	★	★		
Every Other	92		★	★	★
Flash Categories	37		★	★	
Flip the Box	108	★	★	★	★
Frozen Yogurt	65		★	★	★
Funny-Grams	62		★	★	
Geography	54	★	★	★	★
Ghost and Double Ghost	48	★	★	★	★
Gibberish	92		★	★	★
Go-Bang	90		★	★	★
Grandma Is Strange	16		★	★	★

AGE RANGE CHART & INDEX

Game	Page	6–8	8–12	13–18	Adult
Hangman Grows Up	86	★	★		
Hinky Pinky	59		★	★	★
House That Jack Built	78	★	★		
I Love My Love with an A	51	★	★		
I Spy	8	★	★	★	★
License Plate Letters	27	★	★	★	
License Plate Numbers	25	★	★	★	
License Plate Words	27		★	★	
Longest Word	93		★	★	★
Making a Paper Cup You Can Drink From	100	★	★	★	★
Mind Over Money	117		★	★	★
Minister's Cat	70	★	★	★	
Minister's Cat Is All Bad	71		★	★	★
Minister's Cat Will Travel	72		★	★	★
Missing Letter	57		★	★	★
My Grandmother's Trunk	121		★	★	★
My Lady's Lapdog	122		★	★	★
Name That Tune	10		★	★	★
Night Rider	38	★	★		
Number of the Day	30	★	★	★	★
Penny Game	112	★	★	★	
Penny Soccer	105		★	★	
Psychic Experiments	110			★	★
Simplest Solitaire Game	110	★	★	★	★
Snakes	81	★	★		
Snip!	53	★	★		
Sprouts	95		★	★	★
Sugar Game	111	★	★	★	
Super-Ghost	49		★	★	★
Table Football	102		★	★	
Thoughts	69		★	★	★
Tic-Tac-Toe Squared	86		★	★	
Tic-Tac-Toe-Toe	89		★	★	

AGE RANGE CHART & INDEX

Game	Page	Ages 6–8	8–12	13–18	Adult
Travel Songs	40	★	★	★	★
Twenty Questions	11		★	★	★
Ultimate Memory Game	124		★	★	★
Underhand Slap	76	★	★	★	★
Who Are You?	14		★	★	★
Woollcott Game	63		★	★	★
Word Associations	120		★	★	★
Word Bridges	98		★	★	★
Word Steps	94		★	★	★
Word Strings	50		★	★	★
Writing Charades	118		★	★	★
Your Monkey's Moustache	66	★	★	★	★

Hink Pink answers:
1. Large barge
2. Blimp chimp
3. Sick chick
4. Rat chat
5. Coarse horse
6. Glum chum
7. Grim swim
8. Neat beet
9. Sly fly
10. Dull gull

Hinky Pinky answers:
1. Lucky ducky
2. Mighty nightie
3. Gruesome twosome
4. Flirty Gertie
5. Sicker ticker
6. Evil weevil
7. Pocket rocket
8. Chunky monkey
9. Kickin' chicken
10. Noodle doodle

Hinkity Pinkity: A killer gorilla

4-syllable HP: Telly dropped a helicopter